The American Indians and Their Music

By
FRANCES DENSMORE

Collaborator, Bureau of American Ethnology,
Smithsonian Institution, Washington, D. C.

*Author of Chippewa Music, Teton Sioux Music,
Northern Ute Music, Mandan and Hidatsa
Music, etc.*

NEW YORK
THE WOMANS PRESS
MCMXXXVI

Kessinger Publishing's
Rare Mystical Reprints

Thousands of Scarce Books on These and Other Subjects:

Freemasonry * Akashic * Alchemy * Alternative Health * Ancient Civilizations * Anthroposophy * Astrology * Astronomy * Aura * Bible Study * Cabalah * Cartomancy * Chakras * Clairvoyance * Comparative Religions * Divination * Druids * Eastern Thought * Egyptology * Esoterism * Essenes * Etheric * ESP * Gnosticism * Great White Brotherhood * Hermetics * Kabalah * Karma * Knights Templar * Kundalini * Magic * Meditation * Mediumship * Mesmerism * Metaphysics * Mithraism * Mystery Schools * Mysticism * Mythology * Numerology * Occultism * Palmistry * Pantheism * Parapsychology * Philosophy * Prosperity * Psychokinesis * Psychology * Pyramids * Qabalah * Reincarnation * Rosicrucian * Sacred Geometry * Secret Rituals * Secret Societies * Spiritism * Symbolism * Tarot * Telepathy * Theosophy * Transcendentalism * Upanishads * Vedanta * Wisdom * Yoga * *Plus Much More!*

DOWNLOAD A FREE CATALOG
AND
SEARCH OUR TITLES AT:

www.kessinger.net

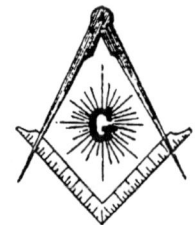

SIYAKA, A SIOUX SINGER

Contents

	PAGE
INTRODUCTION	7
TRIBES AND SOCIAL ORGANIZATION	9
HOME LIFE	15
LANGUAGES	20
ARTS AND CRAFTS	24
CEREMONIES	30
DANCES	37
GAMES	40
MOUNDS AND THE MOUND-BUILDERS	44
EARLY CONTACT OF THE INDIAN AND THE WHITE MAN	47
FAMOUS INDIANS	50
A POPULAR VIEW OF INDIAN SONGS	60
WHY DO INDIANS SING?	63
WORDS OF INDIAN SONGS	68
CHILDREN'S SONGS	74
SONGS BELONGING TO INDIVIDUALS	79
LOVE SONGS	86
MUSICAL INSTRUMENTS	93
WIND INSTRUMENTS	95
DRUMS	102
DRUMSTICKS	109
RATTLES	112
HISTORY OF THE STUDY OF INDIAN MUSIC	121
SOME RESULTS OF THE STUDY OF INDIAN MUSIC	131
CERTAIN PECULIARITIES OF INDIAN MUSIC	134
SCALE IN INDIAN MUSIC	143
ADAPTATIONS OF INDIAN MUSIC	147

List of Illustrations

Śiyaka, a Sioux Singer . . . . *Frontispiece*

                                                              PAGE

1. Piegan Ceremony 35
2. Courting Whistle and Dance Rattle 98
3. Large Decorated Drum 105
4. Ute Indian with Notched Stick Rattle 118

    Photographs of Śiyaka and of musical instruments by courtesy of the Bureau of American Ethnology, Smithsonian Institution.

List of Songs

                                                              PAGE

1. Pawnee Song of Thankfulness 34
2. Cocopa Song of the Bird Dance 39
3. Ute Hand Game Song 42
4. Menominee Moccasin Game Song 43
5. Chippewa Lullaby 74
6. Sioux Song Belonging to Sitting Bull 85
7. "You May Go on the Warpath" (Sioux) 88
8. Chippewa Love Song 91

[6]

Introduction

MUSIC is closely intertwined with the life of every race. We understand the people better if we know their music, and we appreciate the music better if we understand the people themselves. A portion of this book is devoted to the history and customs of the Indians, and a portion to their music in its various phases, but the chief purpose of the book is to assist an acquaintance with our nearest neighbor—the American Indian.

In presenting this material the writer acknowledges the courtesy of the Bureau of American Ethnology of the Smithsonian Institution in permitting the use of data from her unpublished work on the music of many tribes, as well as from her books on Indian music published by that Bureau.[1] The *Handbook of American Indians North of Mexico,* published by the Bureau of American Ethnology, has been consulted in preparing the general chapters concerning the Indians.

---

[1] Chippewa Music, Bulletin 45; Chippewa Music II, Bulletin 53; Teton Sioux Music, Bulletin 61; Northern Ute Music, Bulletin 75; Mandan and Hidatsa Music, Bulletin 80; Papago Music, Bulletin 90; Pawnee Music, Bulletin 93; Menominee Music, Bulletin 102; Yuman and Yaqui Music, Bulletin 110, Bur. Amer. Ethn.; Music of the Tule Indians of Panama, Smithsonian Misc. Coll., Vol. 77, No. 11; and Cheyenne and Arapaho Music, Southwest Museum Papers No. 10. Southwest Museum, Los Angeles, California.

Tribes and Social Organization

ONE of the first questions asked concerning the Indians is, "How many tribes are there?" The name of the Hopi is familiar on account of the Snake dance; we know the Sioux by their valor, and the Osage by their wealth, but few of us would attempt to enumerate the three hundred and forty-two tribes with which the Office of Indian Affairs is dealing, this number "not including sub-tribes and rancheria."

Among the Indians, a tribe was based upon kinship ties and was organized socially and politically. In some tribes this organization was more elaborate than in others and, generally speaking, the organization was simpler in tribes that did not practise agriculture. The highly organized tribes consisted chiefly of the Pueblos, Navaho, and those living in the Atlantic and Gulf states. Among the Plains Indians the Omaha had a highly organized social system, and other Plains tribes of the Siouan family probably were organized in the same manner. The social organization of the western and northern Algonkian tribes is not well known. A majority of the tribes with particularly simple organization is found in the north and along the Pacific coast. The sea-hunting and fishing tribes of the north lived in villages, and among these tribes the heads of houses, together with the village chief, constituted the ruling power. This was a paternalistic government, and the simpler the organization, the more despotic became the power of the chief. Strange as it may seem, the factor of wealth was most important under this régime and the caste system was prevalent. The "first families" could do certain things that were not permitted among the lower classes. These families of course possessed wealth. Their poor relations acted as servants, and they also had numerous slaves, captured in war. A highly organized tribe had a definite system of relationship groups known to ethnologists as clans and gentes. If descent and inheritance were reckoned through the mother, the group of relations was called a clan; if through the father, it was called a gens, and all the members of a group had the same name, usually that of a bird or animal. Thus a man might say he belonged to the wolf clan or the bear clan and anyone would know who were his relatives. On the northwest coast this relationship was expressed by carvings on the totem poles. There were three, ten, or twelve such groups in a tribe. Persons in the same clan or gens were not allowed to marry, as they were supposed to be related by blood, and this rule was strictly enforced.

In highly organized tribes these clans or gentes were grouped in two parts (phratries) which, among the Plains people, camped on opposite sides of the tribal circle. Chieftainship was hereditary in some tribes, while in other tribes it was not inherited; but in all tribes there seems to have been opportunity for a man to attain high rank by wealth and force of character. There were two distinct classes of chiefs, the civil and the military. For example, the Iroquois and the Creeks had civil chiefs and sub-chiefs who were chosen for personal merit out of specified clans or families, and they had both temporary and permanent war chiefs who generally owed their position to merit only. The Iroquois also had chiefs who were elected for their

TRIBES AND SOCIAL ORGANIZATION

merit and statesmanship and who could have no successors in office. These men were called by a name meaning "the solitary pine trees." The Iroquois women alone had the suffrage in their respective family groups, and one woman in each group held the office of chieftainess and "trustee." The Zuni were governed by six rain priests and two war priests, who appointed all the civil rulers. The Indians rarely had rulers corresponding to kings or emperors, and the man thus designated by the early settlers of this country was often a chief who, at that time, was acting as chairman of a council of chiefs.

Four or more tribes sometimes combined in a political league or confederation with a federal council. The most notable example of a union of tribes is the League of the Iroquois, who lived chiefly in the state of New York. The league consisted of the Mohawk, Oneida, Onandaga, Cayuga and Seneca. The Creek Confederacy lasted for more than two centuries and comprised tribes which spoke six languages, the most familiar of these tribes being the Muskogee and Shawnee. The well known Creek war (the only revolt of the Creeks against the Americans) took place in 1813-1814 and ended with the removal of these tribes from Alabama and Georgia to the west, where they were eventually settled in the present state of Oklahoma. The Delaware Confederacy, known as the Lenape, occupied the entire basin of the Delaware River and the adjoining territory, and was prominent in colonial history. These were the only political unions with a tendency toward the formation of a state. The Powhatan confederacy was a union by conquest of the tribes of tide-water Virginia; and King Philip's confederacy, in New England, though short lived, was remarkably destructive. It is said that, of ninety towns, fifty-two were attacked by his warriors and twelve were destroyed. The Chippewa, Ottawa and Potawatomi had an alliance; the Dakota people had their "seven council fires"; and both the Blackfoot and the Caddoan tribes had confederacies, but these were loosely formed organizations, held together by religious or temporary affiliations.

The simplest method of grouping Indian tribes for consideration is by the "culture areas" in which they live. These are about nine in number and comprise the following: (1) Northeast Woodland, (2) Southeast Woodland, (3) Southwest Region, (4) Plains, (5) Plateau, (6) California, (7) Northwest Coast, (8) Northwest Tundra, and (9) Arctic tribes.

Certain tribes were recognized as having definite characteristics developed in part by the territory in which they lived. Among the agricultural tribes were the Mandan, Arickara, Pawnee, Choctaw, Iroquois, Pueblo, and all the tribes of the Piman family, the last two groups having practised irrigation of their fields long before the coming of the white man. Among the "constant fighters" were the Crow, Blackfoot, Comanche, Apache, Cheyenne, Sioux, Creek, Chickasaw and Osage, as well as the Pawnee and Iroquois. The Chippewa and Shoshone are known as especially expert in "medicine" or magic practices. The Nez Percé have always borne a high reputation for independence and bravery and have been noted for almost constant friendliness to the white people. In contrast to this tribe, the Apache have been hostile ever since they appeared on the pages of history.

The term "pueblo" includes several tribes belonging

TRIBES AND SOCIAL ORGANIZATION

to four language groups or linguistic stocks, who are thus combined because they seem always to have lived in compact settlements. These four language groups are the Tanoan, Keresan, Zunian and Shoshonean. The Spanish, who visited the region known as New Mexico before the middle of the sixteenth century, gave them the name "pueblo" which means "town." The most familiar of these tribes are the Zuni and Hopi. The Navaho have lived in the vicinity of the Pueblo Indians but are distinct from them, being stock raisers instead of agriculturists. The Pueblo tribes differ somewhat in their customs. Those living in the north had the "cliff dwellers" as their ancestors, while the forefathers of those living in the valley built a type of many-roomed dwelling, the best example being the present Zuni pueblo near Gallup, New Mexico. This group of Indians practised irrigation of their fields at a remote period of history; they also understood the weaving of cotton cloth and the making of pottery and baskets. Their government was by a priesthood and they were gentle, industrious people.

The cliff dwellers were, in part, the ancestors of the Pueblo tribes and lived at least a portion of the year in many-roomed dwellings which were either hollowed out of rock or built with masonry on high ledges of rock. Some of these dwellings have been excavated and restored, chiefly by Dr. Jesse Walter Fewkes of the Smithsonian Institution. Among the ruins thus restored are those known as Square Tower House, Fire Temple House, Spruce Tree House and Painted Kiva House, in the Mesa Verde National Park.

It is difficult to compare the tribes of Indians with respect to physical characteristics. The Pueblo people, in general, are small in stature, while the Plains tribes comprise many men of unusually large stature. Certain tribes in the southern part of the United States are more reddish in color than those in the northern regions. The tribes that were highly organized and least harassed by war were generally able to acquire greater skill in the native arts, but it is not practical to designate any tribes as being more "artistic" or "intellectual" than others.

Home Life

THE position of women among the Indians has been greatly misunderstood. This is natural, as the early observers of Indian customs came from Europe in the age of chivalry. At that time the feudal system had provided servants for people of wealth, and the frequent wars had placed around women an atmosphere of romance. Nothing could be more widely different than the social conditions in Europe and those among both colonists and Indians in America. The wives of the colonists were hard-working women and expected to share with men the hardships of their new mode of life, but the terms "kings, queens and princesses" had been applied to Indians and could not easily be freed from their accustomed meaning. A queen in Europe did not work, but the wife of an Indian "king" frequently carried on her back the material for an entire dwelling; it appeared, therefore, that she was no better than a slave.

In the old days, an Indian woman might be seen toiling along with a heavy load of camp equipment and, perhaps, with a baby on her back, while her husband, tall and vigorous, walked in front of her. He did not do this because of any lack of respect or affection but in order to "make the way safe" for her. How could a man defend his wife and himself against an ambushed enemy if he carried a kettle in each hand and a pack on his back?

The military spirit dominated Indian society except in settled communities like the Pueblo. A village or camp must be ready for defense and the men must frequently take the warpath to avenge the death of a kinsman or some depredation by the enemy. At certain seasons of the year it was necessary for the men to be absent for weeks or even months while hunting or trapping. A woman's position in the economic life was that of a sharer of work. She had her part to perform, and a man, when free from his own task, was not expected to assume any part of her duties. The men, as already stated, fought the battles and hunted the game; they also made and administered the laws, treated the sick, conducted the religious ceremonies and kept in their memories the tribal histories and rituals, the latter a task of more magnitude than we can realize. The bows and arrows and other articles of wood were made by the men in their leisure hours. Fishing was usually a woman's task and she dried or smoked fish, meat and berries, tanned hides for clothing or other uses, wove mats and blankets, made baskets and pottery, working in every material except wood. It was supposed that seeds would grow better if sowed by women, so in agricultural tribes the care of the fields was entrusted to them.

Polygamy was common if a man could support several wives, and they seem to have lived contentedly. A large number of children was desirable for the future defense of the tribe, and children were expected to work according to their strength and ability. It is the writer's observation that Indian women had a control over their husbands as great as, if not greater than, that of white women. An Indian said: "Marriage among my people was like traveling in a canoe. The man sat in front and paddled the canoe. The woman

HOME LIFE

sat in the stern but she *steered.*" The position of women was highest among the sedentary and highly organized tribes. Thus among the Iroquois and similar tribes the women selected the chiefs and also were elected to that position. Among the Pueblo tribes, a man usually had only one wife, who owned the home and could dismiss him on the slightest provocation. He assisted in domestic work much more extensively than in other tribes, because he was not obliged to go away on war and hunting expeditions. He often made moccasins for his wife, wove blankets and helped gather fuel for the fire. Generally speaking, divorce was an informal matter, often being indicated by the woman's throwing her shoe out of the door.

The child was the strongest bond of the home and was named soon after its birth, frequently receiving a name that was supposed to carry with it the protection of a good spirit. Children had toys made of all sorts of available material and were very fond of pets, especially dogs. The children's games and the stories told to them were intended to train them for adult life, the games developing some quality of mind or body and each story teaching a lesson. Among the Sioux there were special ceremonial acts connected with the piercing of a child's ears, many valuable presents being distributed by wealthy parents at this time. At the age of about twelve years a boy was expected to endure a fasting vigil. This custom seems to have existed, in some form, in every tribe, and the child's parents prepared him by careful instruction. In the Omaha tribe the boy was taught to sing a song as he waited for his vision. The song was recorded by Miss Alice C. Fletcher and the words are translated:

"Wakonda [God], here, poor and needy, I stand."

The young girls did not undergo this fasting vigil, but their passing from childhood was celebrated by ceremonies in many tribes, and they usually married at an early age. They were carefully guarded from too free a friendship with young men, a rather exaggerated shyness being considered the chief charm of an Indian maiden. A young man might blow his "courting flute" in the evening, but no careful mother would allow her daughter to leave the lodge in response to it. The lover must bring the results of the hunt and offer them to the parents before his attentions were recognized. Meantime the young girl was being trained in "domestic art" and became an industrious, intelligent worker, fitted to assume the duties of a new home. As already stated, marriage within the clan or gens was strictly forbidden, as such persons were "blood relations." While marriage customs and requirements differed in the large divisions of the American Indians, there was usually a formality of some sort.

An Indian household usually included three or even four generations, and the old people were highly respected, the children often obeying them more willingly than their parents. If the dwelling were a tent or lodge, there was a definite place for each member of the family, the mother always sitting next the entrance, where she could prepare and dispense the food and also have a knowledge of the comings and goings of all members of the family. The fire was in the center, and the people slept with their feet toward the fire. No children ever played house with more avidity than the Indian children, and the mother encouraged them to imitate her work in their play. As already noted, the children had their little tasks and were proud to have a share in the activities of the family. For example, among the Chippewa the children were given the task of rubbing the strands of bark fiber, making them pliable and ready for the mother's weaving.

The Indian home life seems to have been peculiarly happy except as fear of the enemy might cast its shadow, and the center of the home was the mother, hard working, patient and competent. An important characteristic of Indian women was thrift in the use of household materials. The father's blanket was cut down for the boys until the last smallest pieces were made into caps and mittens; or it was raveled into woolen threads which were twisted into yarn and made into woven bags. The writer once asked an Indian woman to cut a calico dress in the style used by the Indians when they first had cotton cloth. She used the cloth to such good advantage that not a piece was left. The pattern may be described as a plain slip-over with triangular pieces cut from the sides of the skirt and set in the seams above the waist so as to give greater freedom to the arms, and wider shoulders.

Mention should be made of the courtesy of Indians of the higher class. This quality is what we are accustomed to call good breeding and is shown in many ways. A homely example is that of a chief's wife who gave a party for which she made elaborate preparation. When the day arrived I was surprised to see that she wore a very dirty apron. I remarked upon this to a friend, who explained that some of the guests would be untidy and she wished them to feel at ease. The hostess was resolved that at her party no guest should wear an apron dirtier than her own.

Languages

CONTRARY to the prevalent idea, the languages of the American Indians are capable of expressing fine shades of meaning; the vocabularies are rich and the grammatical structure is systematic and intricate. There are more than fifty language groups among the Indians north of Mexico, the language of each tribe belonging to one of these groups. In a similar manner the languages of the Old World are classified as Romance, Celtic, Slavic, etc. Many tribes speak a dialect of a language, this dialect being related to the language as Andalusian is to Spanish, or "Low Dutch" to German. The largest language group is the Algonkian, which includes the Ojibwa (commonly known as Chippewa), Menominee, Delaware, Shawnee and many other tribes. Next in size are (1) the Shoshonean, including Shoshone, Hopi and Ute, and (2) the Siouan, which includes the Dakota (commonly called Sioux), the Winnebago, Omaha and other Plains tribes. Dr. Franz Boas states that in every language "there are a couple of thousands of stem words and many thousand words, as that term is defined in English dictionaries."

Each language group has its own peculiarities, and tribes belonging to one of these groups cannot understand the speech of another. The Algonkian group is characterized by broad smooth vowels, like *a* in "father," and *e* in "they." The Shoshonean group uses the sounds of *u, v* and *w* with frequency, as in the Ute word *uvwiuv* which means song, the consonants being pronounced as in English, with *u* as in "rule" and *i* as in "marine." The languages spoken on the northwest coast abound in the use of *k* and *l* pronounced in a peculiar manner, as in the Makah word *kloklali;* they also use a sound like that of *ch* in the Scotch word "loch." A peculiarity not found in English is a form of language for men and another for women. Among some of the Eskimo this is indicated simply by a difference in pronunciation, but in many tribes the women employ one set of particles and the men use another. Many languages combine several words to form one very long word, really describing an object in detail. Such words are readily formed to indicate something unfamiliar. An example of dialects is offered by the Sioux; the Santee, or southern portion of the tribe, use the letter *d,* while the Teton use the letter *l* in the same words. Thus a Santee Sioux says *koda* (friend) while a Teton says *kola*. There are, of course, other differences in the two dialects.

Many languages are almost obsolete but it has been possible to classify certain tribes by the few remaining words, as the same words, or forms of them, are found in other dialects. Certain tribes have medicine songs in a language that is not understood by the people and is said to be a "dream language." These songs were received in a supposedly supernatural manner, and the experience seems to have been akin to the "speaking with tongues" claimed by primitive prophets.

The nearest approach to a universal language is the sign language, which resembles the gesture language of the deaf. This was formerly understood by all the Plains tribes and enabled strangers to communicate easily with one another. The habit of sign-talking became so natural that Indians of the Plains tribes frequently sign as they converse, keeping their hands in almost constant motion. The use of the hands in sign language is very easy and graceful.

For the Indian skilled in sign language it was natural and easy to draw pictures (pictographs) upon bark, stone or skin, but, according to William H. Holmes, "the evolution of pictographs into sound signs or a true phonetic alphabet must have been very slow. . . . On this continent, so far as known, this stage of thought-writing had been reached only by the Aztec and Maya. . . . Among the Indians of the United States the use of picture signs reached highest development among the Kiowa and the Dakota tribes in their so-called calendars." Pictures on rocks are common over most of North America. According to Mr. Holmes these are not idle scrawls, neither has it been proved that they are "a mine of information respecting the customs, origin and migration of ancient peoples." Frequently they are records of the visits of individuals to certain places, or messages of various sorts, and their significance is chiefly local in character.

The songs and teachings of the Chippewa Grand Medicine Society (Midewiwin) are recorded by means of drawings (mnemonics), understood only by members of the society. So exact is this system that a member of the society, on being shown a song-drawing, can sing the song, while widely separated members of the society draw the same picture on hearing a phonograph record of a melody. These song-pictures are in sets of ten, drawn on strips of birch bark. The design on the title page of this book represents a song of the Chippewa Grand Medicine Society and is the seventh in a series of nine songs used in the initiation of members into the sixth degree of the society.[2] These drawings were made and the corresponding songs phonographically recorded by Debwawendunk, a member of the society living on the Bois Fort reservation in Minnesota. The words of this song were translated, "Diligently listen to those who speak," and the drawing shows the speaker and the listener. The same system is used in records of the society and may be used for proper names.

An alphabet of the Cherokee language was invented by Sequoya and was in use a century ago.

---

[2] Chippewa Music, Bulletin 45, Bureau of American Ethnology, song 22, p. 61, also pp. 15-17.

Arts and Crafts

THE primary handicraft of the Indians consisted in making tools. With implements of wood, stone and bone the Indian prepared materials, built his dwelling and made his household utensils, clothing and weapons. The materials he used were naturally the materials provided by the region in which he lived, and the success of his work depended upon his industry. Tribes varied in proficiency and naturally the tribes that moved about the most or were constantly at war developed the least skill in arts and crafts.

Pottery and basket making are the most familiar Indian arts. To these should be added weaving of various sorts, work with porcupine quills and, after the coming of the trader, a skillful use of beads. Basketry is the most primitive of these arts, as the materials were most generally available. Like all the work which we call artistic, it is done chiefly by the women, and a crude form of agriculture is seen in their care of the plants needed for making baskets. The Indian women are very discriminating, and select the best roots, stalks, grasses and reeds, gathering them at the proper time, storing them in such a manner that they will not become brittle, and combining the materials with a view to the beauty and strength of the finished article. Baskets are used for gathering, carrying and storing materials; they are tightly woven for carrying water and for cooking; they serve as trays for mixing bread, are inverted and pounded as drums, and in some northern tribes are worn as hats. In size they vary from the

ARTS AND CRAFTS

huge storage basket of the Pima, about seventy inches in diameter, to tiny baskets about the size of a thimble. Eight different "stitches" or methods of weaving are used. The baskets of some tribes show symbolic designs in colors, the Hopi excelling in the use of colors. A variety of dyes is used by the Indian women, who in some instances chew a bark with colored juice and dye the basket-splints by drawing them between their lips. Flat basketry was used in the making of houses, shields, clothing, cradles, and for the disposal of the dead. The Hopi made ceremonial masks of basketry, with appendages of hair, feathers and other material. The art was well-nigh universal but the finest weaving was done by the tribes of the southwest and those living on the northwest coast.

Pottery is not so general as basketry because the materials are harder to obtain. Like basketry and weaving, it is a woman's art, and the product of one tribe differs from that of its neighbor. The two large centers of pottery making were the Pueblo region of the southwest and the mound region of the Mississippi valley and the Gulf states. At the present time it is cultivated chiefly by the tribes of New Mexico and Arizona. In making primitive pottery the clay was mixed with various materials such as sand, pulverized stone or shells, the shapes were worked chiefly by hand, and the baking was done in fires or crude furnaces. The process of making a jar often consisted in shaping a round piece of clay for the base and then laying a long rope of clay round and round on the edge of this until the vessel was the desired height, the various coils being molded together by the hands. Sometimes a pattern was made by pressing woven basketry against the moist clay, sometimes "paddle stamps" were used, and in many instances a glaze was applied and patterns were painted in colors. The orange ware of the Hopi was particularly beautiful. Pottery was used for utensils of every sort, for whistles and vases, and also for burial urns by southwestern tribes who cremated the dead.

The two tribes famous for their blanket weaving are the Navaho and the Chilkat. In the latter tribe it was customary to mix shredded cedar bark with goat's wool for weaving the ceremonial blankets, which are a marvel of spinning, weaving, fringing and symbolic design. It is probable that the Navaho, with the Hopi and Zuni, received sheep and looms from the Spaniards as early as the sixteenth century. They learned to card the wool and spin yarn, but the yarn for their finest blankets was obtained by raveling a Spanish cloth called *bayeta*. Symbolic designs were woven in blankets, and many sorts of expert weaving were done, such as making a double-face fabric with different patterns on the two sides. It is interesting to note that the Hopi bridegroom wove a long, elaborate sash for his bride. For a number of years the native dyes were displaced by coal-tar dyes but the influence of the government and various benevolent organizations has encouraged a return to the beautiful native colorings.

Indians delight in color and were able to gratify their taste for bright hues before the coming of the white man. Paints of one class were obtained chiefly from iron-bearing minerals such as ochers and from stained earths. These furnished various tints such as brown, red, green, blue, yellow, orange and purple. White was obtained from kaolin, limestone and gypsum; black was obtained from graphite, powdered coal,

ARTS AND CRAFTS

charcoal or soot; green and blue came from copper ores. An active search was made for new sources of good colors and a commerce in paint materials was carried on among the tribes. The minerals were usually ground in small mortars or rubbed down on a flat stone, and the resultant powder was carried in a small buckskin bag. This powder was mixed with grease before applying to the face or body, and it was mixed with sand for use in the "sand-painting" of the Pueblo tribes. Water and oil were also used in the preparation of paints. The mixing was frequently done in a flat shell and the paint applied with a spongy bone taken from the knee joint of a buffalo or ox. Rude brushes were made of wood, bark or reeds, a small strip being chewed at one end and pounded until soft enough to carry the color.

A great variety of vegetable substances was used in making dye, the formulæ collected by the writer frequently containing several ingredients. Among the plants and trees used by the Chippewa in dye are the puccoon, bloodroot, hazel, sumac, alder, hemlock and butternut, in some instances the root or stalk being used, but more frequently the inner bark supplying the material desired.

Embroidery was an early art of Indian women, the decorations being placed chiefly upon birch bark and hide. The Cheyenne, Arapaho and Sioux women excelled in embroidery with porcupine quills, and beautiful work of this sort was done by the northern Algonkian tribes. The split quills of bird feathers and, among the Eskimo, the hair of the moose, were used in a similar manner. Both the quills and moose hair were dyed and the work, briefly described, consisted in pricking two holes in the material to be decorated, tucking one end of the quill in each hole and cutting off the ends on the wrong side of the material. Some of this work was done with marvelous skill. At length the traders brought beads, and the porcupine quill industry began to languish. Beads were much easier to use and required no preparation. The women of the Plains tribes sewed their beads upon hide, using fine sinew for this purpose but other tribes used cotton thread, obtained from the trader. From a careful investigation, it appears that all the early patterns used by the Chippewa were conventional and that free floral patterns were a later development. The public is somewhat familiar with these decorative patterns but the old designs, with their repose, balance and beauty, must be sought in museums.

Carving in wood, bone, ivory and slate is an art peculiar to the northwest coast. The Eskimo have a genius for carving ivory and bone, while the Haida, Tlingit and neighboring tribes excel in wood carving, as shown in their totem poles, boxes, dishes, rattles, pipes and ceremonial masks. These carvings are symbolic, representing mythical beings as well as the whale, frog, raven, eagle and other forms of animal life. They are painted chiefly in red, yellow and black. The masks frequently are three feet long and represent the head of a bird with a long beak.

The Indian possessed some knowledge of work in metal but did not understand smelting. The metals used were copper, hematite and meteoric iron, lead in the form of galena, nugget gold and mica. Indian craftsmanship consisted in grinding the ores, mixing, rubbing, cold-hammering, engraving, embossing and

ARTS AND CRAFTS

overlaying with plates. The Navaho are expert workers in silver.

The ancient people of Mexico were experts in the art of mosaics and excellent examples of their work have been found as far north as New Mexico. These articles are simple in form and design, usually consisting of pendants to be hung from the ears or attached to a necklace. The foundation is of shell, wood, bone, jet or stone, and the matrix is formed of gum or asphaltum. Turquoise is the favorite material for the inlay but bits of shell or bright-colored stones are also used in making the design.

Ceremonies

INDIAN tribes varied in the number and importance of their ceremonies, the tribes that lived in permanent dwellings being most highly organized and having the most elaborate ceremonies. Thus, generally speaking, the Pueblo people and the tribes that lived in earth lodges had more elaborate ceremonies than the tribes living in birch bark lodges and in tipis. The permanent dwelling was favorable to the keeping of ceremonial articles, and a settled abode gave better opportunity for the memorizing of the rituals that are essential to a long ceremony. Practically all tribes have certain ceremonial acts, such as those connected with the preparing of medicines or the naming of a child, but these are performed by one person or a small number of persons and are not ceremonies in the full sense of the word. A true ceremony is "an expression of religious feeling" and generally refers in some manner to the food supply, either the ripening or harvesting of crops or the securing of meat. Thus the buffalo ceremony was held by the Plains tribes in order that they might secure buffalo, which constituted their most important article of food. Such a ceremony has two parts, one of which is secret and the other public; it also has its priests and its altar with ceremonial articles. It has a ritual which must be recited, songs which must be sung, and a definite reason for its existence. Among many southwestern tribes the secret rites are conducted in underground rooms called kivas; among other tribes the secret rites include fasting, offerings to the gods, and sweat lodge purifications. An event of this part of a ceremony is the search of the priests for the raw material to be used in making the altar. In the Sun dance this is represented by the search of the leaders for the Sun dance pole on which effigies of men and buffalo are hung as offerings. To the uninitiated the leaders appear simply to go into the woods, cut down a tree with some formality and bring the trunk of the tree to the camp, but to the initiate their every action is symbolic.

Between the time of the secret and the public rites there occurs the construction of the place for the ceremony, which usually is circular in form, often symbolizing the earth or the heavens. In this enclosure the altar is placed. This may consist of a buffalo skull decorated with red paint or it may be exceedingly elaborate, as among the Hopi and other Pueblo, whose altars are an assembly of many objects, including "prayer sticks" arranged near a dry sand-painting. The "sacred bundle" of the Pawnee and other tribes is a form of altar, containing sacred articles which are shown only at ceremonies taking place at stated intervals. The writer was permitted to enter the lodge during the Morning Star ceremony of the Pawnee and to see the contents of the sacred bundle. It is said that only one other white person has been given this privilege.

The public part of a ceremony is usually begun with a stately procession of the priests, and includes the reciting of rituals, the singing of prescribed songs and the performance of ceremonial acts, in accordance with the purpose of the ceremony. It is not unusual for a ceremony to last several days, and for a ritual to require many hours for its recitation. The words of the rituals are highly poetic. Among the notable studies of rituals are those of the Omaha and Pawnee by Miss Alice C. Fletcher, and of the Osage by Francis La Flesche. Such ceremonies were attended by the entire tribe and were events of greatest importance.

A dance is one of the most important features of the public portion of a ceremony, the dance being dignified in character and the dancers appropriately costumed.

The Sun dance is a ceremony formerly held at midsummer by tribes of the Plains, including the Sioux, Crow, Ponca and Omaha, Pawnee, Shoshone and Ute. The most prominent element in this ceremony was the dramatic, while in the Morning Star ceremony of the Pawnee and similar ceremonies of other tribes the most important element was ritualistic. At a Sun dance certain men permitted themselves to be suspended by thongs attached to their flesh, this being done in fulfilment of vows made in time of distress or danger. While suspended in this manner they danced, looking steadfastly at the sun, and continued until released by the tearing of their flesh. It is said that, in its symbolism, "the ceremony may be regarded as one of rebirth or reanimation." To the Indian it represented the deepest religious feeling, but it was not understood by the white man; the physical suffering created an unpleasant impression and attracted the morbidly curious, and the discontinuance of the ceremony was ordered by the government. The songs of the Sioux Sun dance were recorded by the writer.

The Snake dance of the Hopi is a noteworthy ceremony which is celebrated as a prayer for rain. It is held every two years, about August twentieth, and is preceded by secret rites which require eight days. These rites are held in underground kivas and include the collecting and washing of the snakes to be carried in the ceremony, the making of the sand altar, and, on the last day, the holding of races and a dance by the Snake fraternity. In the public portion of the ceremony the snake dancers advance in groups of three and each receives a living snake, which he holds by the middle in his mouth. Carrying it thus he dances four times around the plaza and then drops it at an appointed place. He at once repeats the performance with another snake. The ceremony closes with feasting and games.

The Ghost dance was a ceremonial religious dance which originated among the Paiute Indians of Nevada about 1888 and spread rapidly to other tribes. The prophet of this religion was a young man named Wovoka, who claimed to have gone to the spirit world and received a revelation concerning a messiah who would restore the Indians to their former manner of life. Among the Sioux in Dakota the Ghost dance was an important factor leading to the battle of Wounded Knee in 1890. Mr. James Mooney states: "The belief in the coming of a messiah, or deliverer, who shall restore his people to a condition of primitive simplicity and happiness, is probably as universal as the human race. . . . Within the United States nearly every great tribal movement originated in the teaching of some messianic prophet."

A Pawnee ceremonial song is here presented, the

words meaning: "I stand here before you with the Hako" [all the symbolic objects peculiar to the ceremony].

No. 1

PAWNEE SONG OF THANKFULNESS [3]
From HAKO Ceremony

The Piegan ceremony shown in Illustration 1 was witnessed and photographed by Roland Reed in northern Montana, in 1911. No detailed description of the ceremony is available but Mr. Reed states that it was of a deeply religious character. The leader was Many Tail Feathers, who is seen carrying a feathered object at the head of the procession. The drummer nearest the center of the picture is Stabs-by-mistake, next to him is Eagle Ribs, and the third in the line is Two Guns. These men are also the singers. Mr. Reed states further that these people call themselves the "underwater people," and in preparation for this ceremony they visited a lake carrying a forked pole which they put under the water. The procession illustrated came

---

[3] Fletcher, Alice C., *The Hako: A Pawnee Ceremony.* Twenty-second Report, Bureau of American Ethnology, p. 177.

ILLUSTRATION 1.—PIEGAN CEREMONY

to the tent at the extreme left of the picture where a "medicine bundle" was unwrapped, the removal of each wrapper being attended by ceremonial action. It required several days for the preparations but the ceremony was concluded in one day and was exceedingly impressive.

Dances

THE importance of the dance in the life of the Indian is shown by the fact that his most elaborate ceremonies are commonly known as dances. Many of the oldest dances of the Indians were symbolic or ceremonial in character, and dancing was always associated with the departure of the warriors and their victorious return. In certain tribes the dancers imitated birds and animals, and it was customary for a warrior to act out his exploits when dancing the war dance. There were dances for both men and women; other dances in which men or women danced by themselves; and others in which individuals danced alone. There were comic dances, and dances in costumes that disguised the persons taking part. There was dancing when the period of mourning for the dead was terminated, and dancing when the mysterious Medicine Lodge held its meetings. In some dances the action was violent and in others the people "danced standing still," simply flexing their knees and rising up and down. In some dances the motion was sideways, the dancers standing in a circle and moving east to west ("with the sun"), or in the opposite direction; while in other dances they stood in long rows facing each other and moved a few steps forward and backward or walked in a manner resembling the old-fashioned grand march. The dances of great activity were limited to the men, whose contortions in some of them seemed to bring into play every muscle of their bodies and limbs. Generally speaking, a woman danced with head so quietly erect that it seemed as though she might have carried a water-jar on her head as she danced. Her arms often wrapped her shawl closely around her body, and the only motion was a short step to the side, with one foot after another. The Makah had a great number of what we would call interpretative dances, and it was not unusual for a woman to dance alone; while in a majority of other tribes this custom is unknown.

The dances were many, but each dance had its name, its step and movement of the dancers, and its special songs; it also had its history and, frequently, its symbolism. Dances acquired from other tribes were credited to their sources. The songs were usually sung by the men, who played the accompanying instruments. If the dancers moved in a circle, the accompanying instruments were placed in the middle of the circle; otherwise they were in a row at one side.

The accompaniment for dances usually consisted of singing and playing on instruments of percussion. The singers were men and their voices took the place of the higher, melody-playing instruments of a band or orchestra, while the percussion instruments supplied the rhythm. In some tribes and in some classes of songs the women sang with the men, singing an octave higher. The instruments of percussion are described in the chapters on drums and rattles. Whistles were sometimes blown while dancing was in progress but cannot be regarded as accompanying instruments.

The foregoing represents the old custom, and does not take into consideration the dancing of Indians at the present time.

The following is a song of the Bird dance of the

DANCES

Cocopa Indians, who live near the Mexican border in southwestern Arizona.

No. 2
COCOPA SONG OF THE BIRD DANCE [4]

[4] *Yuman and Yaqui Music,* Bulletin 110, Bureau of American Ethnology, No. 101.

[39]

Games

IN the playing of games the Indian developed and used three faculties that were important in his daily life; these were quickness of hand, keenness of observation and the ability to make a good guess—which is nothing more than a quick decision. He had no games that required deliberation, like checkers or chess. In the old days, gambling was considered a legitimate means of obtaining wealth, and the ability to win was regarded as a gift from the spirits. The betting ran high, but if an Indian staked all he possessed on his skill in playing a game it was no greater risk then he took when he went to war. Patience and self-control were also developed through the playing of games. The writer has seen games which had been in progress several hours and in which one side had lost heavily, but from the expression on the faces of the players it was impossible to know which were the losers.

In certain tribes the game implements were symbolic and the games were ceremonial in character. For example, it is still the custom among the Menominee to play a game in fulfilment of a "dream obligation" in order to obtain the benefits promised in the dream.

Two classes of games were played by the Indians; these were (1) games of chance, and (2) games of dexterity. To the former class belong games in which objects resembling dice are thrown and games in which the location of hidden objects is guessed; while to the latter class belong such games as lacrosse, kicked-ball, or the sliding of sticks across the snow. The forms of all these games varied in different tribes. Sometimes the objects resembling dice were marked sticks thrown from the hand, and sometimes they were small carved objects or marked plumstones tossed upward in a bowl or basket, the count depending on the markings that were uppermost when they fell. The hidden objects might be held in the hand or placed under moccasins that were laid on the ground. The most general form was the "hand game" in which two short pieces of bone were concealed in the hands. One of these objects was plain, the other was marked, and the count depended upon guessing the location of the marked piece. Four pieces, one of which was marked, were used in a similar manner. The players were divided into opposing sides and a game was attended by a large number of persons. Such a game among the Pawnee was somewhat ceremonial in character and songs of the Ghost dance were sung during its periods of dancing. In playing the "moccasin game" four metal balls were slipped under four moccasins which were laid in a row on a blanket, one "bullet" being marked. The man who hid them tried to make no sign as he slipped the marked bullet under a moccasin, and his opponents watched for some change of expression when it slipped through his fingers. When the four bullets had been placed, the opponents made their guess, the assistants of the hiding player pounding on their drums and singing lustily. Among southwestern tribes, a grain of corn was hidden in one of four cane tubes and its location guessed in a somewhat similar manner. The four tubes referred to the four world quarters, and the game was sacred to the war gods.

It is said that in general the arrow or the bow, or

some object derived from them, is the predominant implement in Indian games, and a conception of the four world quarters is the fundamental idea. Gaming implements are among the significant objects placed on many Hopi altars. The ball was a sacred object, not to be touched by the hand, and symbolizing the earth, the sun and the moon. In the kicked-ball and ball-race games of the southwest, the primary purpose was to protect the crops from sandstorms within the circuit traversed by the players. Among the Yuma Indians these races were held immediately after the ceremony to secure rain and were considered important events. Among the Menominee, even at the present time, it is believed that the sick may be benefited by attending a lacrosse game when it is played "in fulfilment of a dream." These instances indicate briefly the significance of gaming in the olden times. This significance has now passed away except in a limited number of tribes that still cling to the old beliefs.

No. 3

UTE HAND GAME SONG [5]

---

[5] *Northern Ute Music*, Bulletin 75, Bureau of American Ethnology, No. 98.

GAMES

No. 4
MENOMINEE MOCCASIN GAME SONG [6]

---
[6] Unpublished material, Bureau of American Ethnology.

Mounds and the Mound-Builders

FOR many years the mound-builders were supposed to be a race of men different from the American Indians, but history and archæology have revealed that the building of mounds was simply a custom shared by a number of Indian tribes of different stocks. For example, the mounds in the south were built by the Indian tribes found in the same general region in the sixteenth century. A majority of these tribes now live in other localities but at that time the Cherokee lived in the Appalachian region of Georgia, Tennessee and the Carolinas, the Creeks were in Georgia and Alabama, and the Choctaw, Chickasaw and Natchez were in Mississippi. These and other tribes were sedentary people, living in permanent villages and having substantial houses, and the building of mounds was a phase of their life. Some mounds contain articles of European manufacture, showing them to be comparatively modern. According to Mr. Henry B. Collins, Jr., of the United States National Museum, the origin of mound building is probably traceable to Mexico and Central America, where the highest civilizations of ancient America—the Maya, Toltec and Aztec—were found, their elaborate stone temples resting on large, flat-topped mounds faced with stone.

A few mounds have been found on the Pacific coast but the region in which they abound is that of the Gulf states and the Mississippi basin. The east coast of Florida is dotted with "shell heaps" in which skeletons and pre-Columbian articles are found, but these do not

MOUNDS AND THE MOUND-BUILDERS

indicate a race different from that known as the American Indian. The shell heap was first a mound of refuse but as the material decayed it was sometimes used in making a mound for burial or other purposes.

Aside from refuse heaps, or kitchen middens, and the heaps of earth that cover ruins in the southwest, there are four distinct types or classes of mounds: one was used for burials; one for defense; one for the site of temples, council houses or chiefs' dwellings; and a fourth consisted of effigy mounds which were made in the shape of animals. A typical burial mound is low, broad, and has a rounded top. The smaller ones can scarcely be distinguished from natural mounds and the largest are eighty to one hundred feet high. They are usually in groups, on elevated ground with a particularly fine view of the surrounding country. The mounds for defense were in the form of earthworks, or long walls, from fifty to nine hundred feet long. Some were enclosures in the shape of squares, oblongs or circles, and were so wonderfully planned that in one or two instances a round enclosure a thousand feet in diameter varied less than ten feet from a true circle. The elevated sites for temples, commonly designated as mounds, were flat on the top and often very large. The Cahokia mound in Illinois is one hundred feet high, has two levels with sloping terraces, and covers about sixteen acres. This remarkable mound is about six miles east of St. Louis, Missouri. An explorer who visited it in 1811 recorded that it was "surrounded by forty-five mounds besides a great number of artificial elevations." The largest mound in the south is the Etowah mound in Georgia, located three miles from Cartersville in Bartow County. It is a quadrilateral truncated pyramid sixty-one feet high and the area of the base is a little less than three acres. Archæological evidence seems to indicate that the mound may have been constructed by the ancestors of the Cherokee.

The fourth class of mounds, made as effigies of animals, were usually in groups and varied from fifty to five hundred feet in length. Many mounds of this class are found in Wisconsin.

The pottery found in mounds has contributed to our knowledge of Indian art. Specimens in a good state of preservation are often found in burial mounds, and the pattern of an entire jar or bowl can frequently be constructed from broken fragments. The manner of placing bodies in the ground, and the various articles buried with the dead, have been of great assistance in the study of the American Indian.

Only a very small proportion of the Indian mounds have been opened. Many of the remainder are being leveled by the plow and the information they contain is forever blotted out.

Early Contact of the Indian and the White Man

WHEN the early French, English and Spanish explorers came to this country, they took possession of the land in the name of their sovereigns. The Indians made no objection because they did not think of land as a commodity to be bought or sold. They knew what it meant to be conquered by stronger tribes, and the explorers impressed them with the greatness of their foreign rulers, using a great deal of pomp and ceremony when planting the king's or the queen's standard in the New World. Gifts were exchanged but the transaction differed from a sale.

The Puritans did not come in the name of a sovereign and it was necessary for them to bargain with the Indians in order to obtain land. They treated the Indian chiefs as they would have treated foreign potentates, even calling them "kings," and they gave the name "nation" to tribes which lacked the coherence of an established government. Thus began the custom of negotiation with the Indians, under the assumption that Indian and European concepts of land ownership were the same.

The United States, through its constitution, continued the policy established by the colonies and negotiated with the Indians by solemn treaties, the only difference being that treaties were made by Congress instead of by the individual colonies. This was not set aside until 1871, when the power of making treaties with the Indians was placed under the jurisdiction of the President.

Though a tribe may have been reduced to a small number, the treaty was usually clothed in the same stately verbiage as the most important treaty with a European power. The amount of land involved in a treaty varied greatly but the form was always the same. In the early days an Indian reservation was usually a part of the land transferred to the government by a treaty. A part of the tract was thus reserved for the continued use of the Indians. Other means of establishing reservations are not of present interest.

The individual ownership of land by Indians was made possible by the Severalty Act of 1887, which allotted to each Indian man, woman and child a definite portion of the reservation or other public land. The United States held the allotment in trust for twenty-five years, after which the Indian, if competent to manage his affairs, was given full title to the land. If the Indian were incompetent the trust period was extended. As the allotments among the Plains tribes ranged from eighty to three hundred and sixty acres, and as a family often comprised six or more persons it will be seen that a large amount of territory was allotted to the Indians. The Office of Indian Affairs states that "the total area of land allotted to individual Indians as of June 30, 1925, is 39,976,452 acres, of which more than 39,000,000 acres were reservation lands and the remaining or about 960,000 acres were from the public domain." Land owned by Indians is inherited according to the same laws that govern inheritance among members of the white race, and the estate of an Indian is probated by the government with a division of the property among his heirs.

The Bureau of Indian Affairs was organized in 1824 within the War Department, which had been in charge of the general affairs of the Indians since 1789. The change from military to civil administration took place in 1849, when the Department of the Interior was created and the Bureau of Indian Affairs transferred to that department. Its official title is the Office of Indian Affairs.

Famous Indians

AFTER the coming of the white man to America, the Indians who rose to prominence were usually men who distinguished themselves in some form of contact with the colonists, the settlers or the government of the United States. The fields of industry, education, commerce and science in which men now become prominent were then unknown, while war was an honorable occupation. Hence a majority of the Indians accounted as famous were identified with war or with the making of treaties. Unfortunately there have been no native historians to record the lives of these men from the standpoint of the Indian, but a majority of them are recognized as men of strong character, firm convictions and high personal honor, and some were "constructive statesmen" among their own people. Their conflict with the white man was frequently an outgrowth of their ambition for the integrity and safety of their race. Back of the conflict and lost in the silence of the past is the story of their personal leadership in the camp and the council, as well as the benefits they may have secured for their people.

The following list does not include all Indians who have distinguished themselves, but comprises many who are prominent in American history. Monuments to several of these have been erected in eastern and western cities.

Probably the first Indians of whom we have definite traditions are Dekanawida and his associate Hiawatha who lived about 1550. Although Dekanawida was the greater man, it is Hiawatha who is more familiar to the white race, yet few know him in his right character. He was a Mohawk chief whose name meant "he who makes rivers," and he was associated with Dekanawida in planning and founding the League of the Iroquois, which comprised five Iroquois tribes. He also introduced certain reforms among his people which were considered very remarkable. Schoolcraft confused him with Manabozho, the creative deity of the Ojibwa, who is said to have "taught the Indians how to live on the earth," and in this form the Hiawatha legends were received and immortalized by Longfellow.

Soon after the landing of the Pilgrims, in 1670, a chief named Samoset came to them and said, "Welcome English," in their own language. He had sojourned in the Cape Cod country for a few months and acquired this evidence of culture. He introduced the Pilgrims to Massasoit and both were friendly to the white men. A younger son of Massasoit, however, was King Philip, the leading spirit in a long struggle against the English. His Indian name was Metacom and he made havoc in the white settlements, but history accords him a place among heroic warriors.

Powhatan ruled about thirty Indian tribes in Virginia in 1607 and was about sixty years of age when the English came to that region. His first attitude toward the white men was friendly but he became embittered and hostile. His Indian name was Wahunsonacock, the name Powhatan being that of one of his favorite residences near the present site of Richmond. His daughter Pocahontas is one of the few romantic women of Indian history. Her name means "playful," and it is pleasant to think of her as a petted, playful child, who might have saved the life of a white man in the whimsical manner of a child asking a favor from an indulgent, powerful father. Her kidnapping by the British and ransom by her father, as well as her marriage to John Rolfe and death in England are familiar to students of history.

Among other prominent Indians of the Atlantic coast was Cornplanter, son of a white trader and a Seneca woman, who was given 640 acres of land in Pennsylvania "for his many valuable services to the whites." He was more than ninety years old at the time of his death in 1836. At about this time lived Tamanend, the Delaware chief whose name means "the affable one." The fame of his virtues was such that during the Revolutionary War his admirers dubbed him "St. Tammany, the patron saint of America." The celebrations in his honor were the beginning of "Tammany societies," and numerous political and military societies organized on an Indian basis. This custom spread rapidly. The largest society had its headquarters in New York and its meeting place was called the "wigwam." It had a "tribe" in each of the original thirteen states, called by the name of a bird or animal, as the "Eagle tribe," and "Otter tribe."

Black Hoof, the principal chief of the Shawnee, was born about 1740 and led his tribe in a merciless warfare against the white men both east and west of the Allegheny mountains. After his defeat as a warrior he exercised his power as an orator and counselor. When the British tried to stir the Shawnee into rebellion against the government of the United States, Black Hoof held the majority of them in restraint. One whom he could not manage was Tecumseh, who distinguished himself in the border wars and is said to have been the most extraordinary Indian character in the history of the United States. In the War of 1812, he promptly led his men to the support of the British, who gave him a regular commission as a brigadier general, with command over 2,000 Indians. He died in 1831.

The life of Pontiac is an interesting story. He consented to acknowledge King George but only as an "uncle," not as a superior. Failing to receive what he considered a proper recognition, he devised a plan to destroy all the forts and settlements of the British in the region about Detroit. For this undertaking he secured the aid of most of the tribes in Ohio. When this failed he tried to organize the Indians along the Mississippi in an attempt to drive out the British. He finally made peace at Detroit in 1765. It is said that "Pontiac, if not fully the equal of Tecumseh, stands second to him in strength of mind and breadth of competence."

A fourth in this group of Indian warriors was Logan, born in Pennsylvania in 1725. His father was a white man who had been taken a prisoner in Canada, raised among the Indians and later made a chief. A number of his relatives were massacred by the white settlers, and as a result Logan made terrible and barbarous war on the white settlements, boasting of his murders in a speech which made him famous.

One of the greatest Indian orators was Red Jacket, the Seneca, born about 1756. His name in civil life meant "prepared" and his name as a chief meant "he who causes them to be awake," both names seeming to be characteristic of the man. With great reluctance he joined the British during the Revolution and they rewarded him with a bright red jacket, replacing it when it was worn out, until he became known by his present name. He was a vacillating character, not a broadminded thinker. His excellence lay in quick wit, defensive debate, and a most tenacious memory. In 1829, Catlin painted a full-length portrait of him standing on Table Rock, Niagara Falls, this pose being requested by Red Jacket.

As time passed and settlements moved westward, the prominent Indians are found in the Mississippi valley. Keokuk was born in Illinois in 1780. His mother was partly of French descent. He was a man who worked by intrigue and veiled intentions, but his services to the government were of such importance that he was appointed chief of the Sauk tribe. As an orator he was simple and pleasing, and in debate he was always deliberate and clearheaded. Keokuk, as indicated, was friendly to the United States government, but Black Hawk, of the same tribe, was always British in his affiliations. The Black Hawk War was one of the most memorable conflicts between the Indians and the whites, with heavy losses to both races.

It will be noted that many of the Indians thus far described in this chapter became famous by their general attitude toward the British or the colonists. Attention has been called to the fact that Indians held land in common, except as certain members of a community used a definite part of it by common consent. The colonists adopted the idea of kings and queens among the Indians because it simplified the transactions in regard to land. They were thus dealing with an individual, or, in the treaties, with a small group of Indians, but the Indians did not recognize the right of a "king," a group of people, or even a tribe, to sign away the land which was held by several tribes in common. The inevitable result of these sales or gifts was bad feeling. The white people considered the transaction to be legal and the Indians did not, and attempts to enforce the sales were followed by disorder and bloodshed. A majority of the Indians mentioned in the remainder of this chapter were connected with these tribal transfers of land.

William MacIntosh was the son of a Scotch trader and a Creek woman. He was friendly to the whites and held the rank of major in the War of 1812, but in later years his avarice overcame his good judgment. Under pay from the white men he negotiated treaties for Creek land, and continued this policy after the Creeks had passed a law punishing by death any member of the tribe who signed a land treaty. In accordance with this law he was shot by the Creek warriors. His name is on five treaties.

Pushmataha, a Choctaw, born in 1774, distinguished himself as a leader during the War of 1812, carrying the Choctaw to the side of the United States when their friends the Creeks joined the British. Later, in negotiating a land treaty "he displayed much diplomacy and showed a business capacity equal to that of General Jackson, against whom he was pitted, in driving a sharp bargain."

The Comanche tribe had its most distinguished representative in the person of Quanah Parker, the son of a Comanche chief and a captive white woman. After a period of organized warfare against the white men along the southern border of Kansas, he accepted the inevitable. With the intelligence inherited from his ancestors, he soon became a leader of his people in the ways of civilization. Through his influence they leased their surplus pasture land, and in all his guidance of their affairs he showed himself a practical business man.

Another great man of the Indian race was Chief Joseph of the Nez Percé, whose native name meant "thunder coming from the water, up over the land." He was a man of fine presence and high character, and was one of the most remarkable Indians in United States history. Chief Joseph and his band did not recognize the validity of the treaty of 1863 which deprived them of their right to the Wallowa valley in Oregon. Added to this injustice were many outrageous acts on the part of white settlers, and Chief Joseph took the warpath. When retreat became necessary he led his band more than a thousand miles, encumbered by women and children, his military skill pitted against that of Colonel Sturgis, General O. O. Howard and General Nelson A. Miles, with their Indian scouts. His objective point was the Canadian border and he was within fifty miles of it when his progress was cut off by fresh troops and he was captured. In later years he became reconciled to civilization and encouraged the education of the children of his tribe.

The name of Geronimo carries with it a memory of hostility and defiance. The man who bore it was an Apache, born about 1834, and the name is Spanish for Jerome. His native name meant "one who yawns," and he was by profession a medicine man and a prophet. To and fro across the Mexican border he led his band of followers, committing depredations in both countries. After his surrender to General Miles, he was

FAMOUS INDIANS

taken as a prisoner of war to Florida, and finally confined at Fort Sill, Oklahoma, where he died.

Sitting Bull, the noted Sioux chief and warrior, was born in the same year, 1834. As a child he was known as Jumping Badger, later as Tom Horn, and when he had shown skill as a medicine man his name was changed to Sitting Bull. He was on the warpath almost continually from 1869 to 1876, against either the frontier posts or western Indians. At last his refusal to go on a reservation led General Sheridan to begin a campaign with a "fight to the finish." The "Custer massacre" was part of Sitting Bull's resistance to the white man. An account of this battle was given to Major James McLaughlin many years afterward by an Indian woman who took part in it. This interesting narrative ends with the words: "So it was that the Sioux defeated Long Hair and his soldiers in the valley of the Greasy Grass River, which my people remember with regret, but without shame. We are now living happily and in friendship with the whites, knowing that their hearts are good toward us."[7] Sitting Bull and his band escaped to Canada but were brought back. A few years later he went on a reservation but continued unreconciled. His influence was always a disturbing one and he was finally shot by Indian police who were placing him under arrest. He excelled as an organizer, and was honored by his people as a medicine man.

In the same band of the Sioux was a slightly younger chief with a totally different character. This man was Gall, who was a lieutenant of Sitting Bull's at the Cus-

---
[7] McLaughlin, James, *My Friend the Indian*, Houghton Mifflin Company, New York, 1910, p. 177.

ter massacre and fled with him to Canada, but later withdrew from Sitting Bull's band, surrendered to the United States government and settled as a farmer on the Standing Rock reservation in North and South Dakota. He was a man of noble presence and high character, respected by white men as well as by Indians, and his influence was exerted in behalf of the government. In his later years he was a judge of the court of Indian offenses at the Standing Rock agency.

One of the greatest Sioux warriors was Red Cloud, of Pine Ridge, South Dakota, born in 1822, who opposed with armed force the building of a road from Fort Laramie, Wyoming, to the goldfields of Montana. Red Cloud held the opinion that travel over this new road would destroy the best hunting ground of the buffalo. It is interesting to note that his opposition was followed by fighting with troops, by councils, and by a treaty, and that in the end he won the position he had taken at the beginning. During the rest of his life he kept his promise to be loyal to the government, but he never ceased to resist the "new era" of civilization.

Mention should here be made of Sacagawea, the Shoshone woman who accompanied Lewis and Clark on their expedition across the continent. She was a captive among the Hidatsa, who had given her this name, which means "bird woman." Her husband was a French Canadian *voyageur* whom the expedition engaged as interpreter, and the journey promised her an opportunity to return to her own people in the west. Through her aid the explorers obtained ponies from the Shoshone, without which they could not have crossed the divide. In this, as in many other emergencies, she proved herself a woman of resourcefulness and great strength of character.

Only one Indian ever achieved an alphabet of his language. This man was Sequoya, born about 1760, the son of a white man and a mixed-blood Cherokee woman. He invented the Cherokee alphabet in which parts of the Bible were printed in 1824 and a weekly paper in 1828.

This enumeration closes with Smohalla, the prophet and originator of a "religion" which spread rapidly among the tribes of Washington, Oregon and Idaho. He was born about 1815 or 1820, and in his childhood became familiar with the ceremonies of a Roman Catholic mission. After a brief career as a warrior, he took a long journey, going as far south as Mexico. On his return he said that he had been to the spirit world and brought back a message to the Indian race. This message, like that of other aboriginal prophets, was that the Indians must return to their old manner of life, have nothing further to do with the white man, and be guided entirely by the priests of the new cult. The religion of Smohalla thus resembled that of the Ghost dance in some respects, but it had certain ceremonies evidently adapted from those of the Roman Catholic Church. It still has its followers, who hold meetings at stated intervals and are called the Dreamers.

A Popular View of Indian Songs

IT has been flippantly said that Indian music is the pandemonium of a small boy conducted with the dignity of his grandfather. Early explorers wrote that it was not unpleasant when one became accustomed to it, and travelers pausing at an Indian camp have said the Indians seemed to have only one tune which was sung over and over. Tourists have said that Indian music is chiefly rhythmic, and missionaries have regarded it as a persistent phase of heathenism. In most of these observations there is a grain of truth but none is based upon an extended acquaintance with the subject.

An important characteristic of many Indian songs is a descending trend. Sometimes the melody descends steadily from the first note to the last, and sometimes there is an ascent in the middle of the song, after which it resumes its downward trend. Not all songs are made after this pattern, but it is a respect in which Indian songs differ from our own. The next characteristic is a frequent change of measure-lengths. When we begin a song in 3-4 time we usually continue that time throughout the song, but the Indian does not space his accents so evenly. A majority of Indian songs when transcribed in our notation contain triple and double measures alternating in what seems to be an irregular manner with occasional measures of other lengths. Overshadowing all other peculiarities, to a listener of our own race, is a manner of tone-production entirely different from our own and not wholly agreeable to our ears. This is considered further in the chapter on "Certain Peculiarities of Indian Music."

One of the musical requirements of the white race is that a song and its accompaniment shall be "exactly together," but an Indian song may be either a little faster or a little slower than the accompanying drum without disturbing the Indian musicians.

The Indian takes his music seriously and has nothing that corresponds to our popular songs. There are standards of excellence in his music (see page 137) and he practises in order to attain them, although Indians do not have musical performances corresponding to our concerts. The Indians have no melody-producing instruments except the flute, which has its special uses (see page 95), so the voices of the singers around the drum are like the melody-producing instruments in our orchestras or bands, while the drum is like the bass or percussion instruments which supply the rhythm. The singers and the drum or other percussion accompaniment provide the music at all dances and social gatherings as well as at the tribal ceremonies. They have rehearsals, as we do, and practise and learn new songs. If a man goes to visit another tribe he tries to remember and bring home songs, which are always credited to the source whence they came.

The Choctaw have many dances without any accompaniment whatsoever. These dances were witnessed by the writer near Philadelphia, Mississippi, when studying the music of the Choctaw, and have not been noted in any other North American tribe.

Songs are taught to one person by another, and in the old days it was not unusual for a man to pay the value of one or two ponies for a song. He did not buy such a song for his own pleasure but because it had a ceremonial connection or was believed to have magic power. To this class belong the songs for treating the sick and those believed to bring rain.

There are differences in the songs of various tribes, some of which are apparent while others are revealed by the analysis of the songs. One who has lived much among the Indians writes of the "stateliness of Kiowa music, the apparent discord of the Comanche, the interesting way in which one voice leads in the Creeks and others come in apparently as each one wishes, but altogether the volume of sound is harmonious and rises and falls like the waves of the ocean, while the Apache music sounds as if it might have been composed as the people rode over the desert country on their little ponies." In the experience of the present writer, there are contrasts in the various classes of songs within a tribe as well as differences between the songs of certain tribes. In some instances the songs of one class resemble those of the same class in another tribe whose music, in other respects, is quite different. This has been noted concerning game songs and medicine songs. If we make our thought of Indian music broad enough we shall find an unexpected range of interest.

A technical consideration of Indian music is presented in a subsequent chapter.

Why Do Indians Sing?

THE radical difference between the musical custom of the Indian and our own race is that, primarily, the Indians used song as a means of accomplishing definite results. Singing was not a trivial matter, like the flute-playing of the young men. It was used in treating the sick, in securing success in war and the hunt, and in every undertaking which the Indian felt was beyond his power as an individual. An Indian said, "If a man is to do something more than human he must have more than human power." Song was essential to the putting forth of this "more than human power," and was used in connection with some prescribed action. It was usually accompanied by drumming or the shaking of a rattle. Thus it is seen that Indian music (both vocal and rhythmic instrumental) originally lay in the field of what we call religion. It was used chiefly by medicine men, who corresponded to our priests and physicians, and by individuals who had acquired mystic power through dreams and visions. Music was prominent in all Indian ceremonies and was used as a means of securing success in games. Dances were originally a part of ceremonies. In comparatively modern times it became customary to hold social dances at the same time as a ceremony, but at some little distance, so that the two did not conflict. As time passed, the social dances increased in favor, and with the passing of the old religion the ceremonies waned. Men continued to play games but they did not take them quite so seriously. Thus music gradually assumed a more secular character. The conservatism of the medicine men has preserved many old songs, but the young Indians do not care for these songs nor, in a majority of instances, understand their original significance.

The early purpose of Indian music, outlined in the preceding paragraph, has frequently been designated as "calling upon the spirits for help," or "summoning supernatural aid." This is so familiar a concept that we accept it readily, but a more intensive explanation is given by Mr. J. N. B. Hewitt, of the Bureau of American Ethnology. Mr. Hewitt states that Indians believed in a certain spirit indwelling not only in man but in every living creature and in nature. Thus a man who desired "more than human power" would not be seeking something different from what he possessed but would seek to supplement his own power by the addition, or cooperation, of a similar power resident in some other creature or in nature. Mr. Hewitt suggests that the Iroquois word *orenda* be used to designate this universal indwelling spirit. The terms *spirit power, supernatural power* and *medicine power* are in common use. With this knowledge of the Indian's belief we can realize that nothing was supernatural to him, in our use of that term. Nothing was too strange for him to explain by means of this mysterious power which he felt that he shared with all created things. It made the animals his brothers and even the Thunderbird his friend, to whom he could offer tobacco by placing it on the fire and letting the smoke ascend. The words of many Indian songs contain a meaning which is made clear by this knowledge of orenda. For example, a Papago medicine song contains these words:

> A black snake goes toward the west,
> It travels erect on its tail,
> It sings as it goes toward the west,
> It coils around a mountain.

The snake was not singing, as we sing for pleasure, but he was exerting his orenda, which, in animals as in man, is put forth by means of song. A Cocopa song contains the words, "A bush is sitting under a tree and singing," the idea conveyed to the Cocopa being that the bush was putting forth its orenda, or spirit power.

An early form of Indian music consisted of songs interpolated in stories of mythical personages, "creators" and "wonder-workers." The telling of such stories was a serious matter, taking place at definite times and preceded by acts of a ceremonial character. In many of these songs the mythical personages are supposed to be speaking, while other songs tell of their marvelous acts, due to the power of their orenda. Such are the stories of Winabozho (or Manabozho) of the Ojibwa, whose orenda was so great that he changed into an animal or even into the trunk of a tree at his will. In modern times these stories are told simply for amusement, but originally the mythical being was demonstrating the power of his orenda and filling the Indians with awe and wonder.

Mention has been made of the desire of the Indian for an orenda stronger than his own, the purpose being to benefit the tribe or individuals. From this desire arose the ceremonies to produce good crops, to bring rain or to call the animals needed for food. Songs were used in the ceremonies but there were instances in which the singing of a song by an individual was said to produce a marvelous result. When a medicine man began to treat a sick person the result depended on the power of his orenda. Sometimes it was believed that the sickness was caused by the action of a "bad medicine man" who had bewitched the patient, and in such a case the orenda of the doctor was pitted against that of the man who was working bad magic. When a hunter met a bear the result depended not upon physical force but upon which had the stronger orenda, the hunter or the bear. We have no idea similar to this, and it is difficult to describe native concepts in the language of civilization; moreover, Indian tribes differ, and tribes in different stages of advancement show modifications of their original thought, but it is hoped that Mr. Hewitt's explanation may assist an understanding of the early beliefs of the American Indians.

The putting forth of orenda by means of song did not prevent the Indian's attention to material matters. The hunter made his arrow straight although he sang "hunting charm songs," and the warriors were trained for fighting, although they never went to war without a medicine man. It was the duty of the medicine man to locate the enemy and create conditions favorable for the encounter. Thus he might cause a terrific wind to blow, or bring fog or rain, under cover of which an attack could be made effectively. Those who possessed orenda strong enough to do these wonderful things were men of intense concentration; their lives were subject to rigid discipline and they spent much time in fasting and meditation. They were consecrated to their work, believing that on their efforts depended the safety, success and health of their people.

New customs have brought new songs to the Indian but he has not yet adopted the white man's custom of singing for the approval of an audience. Song is still for the benefit of all, and a man desires excellence in singing that he may be a leader of the singers at the drum, not that he may sing alone. The young men are composing songs and frequently adapting Indian melodies for band instruments, but the old songs—the songs of mysterious power—are kept in the hearts of the few who love the old ways and still follow them.

Words of Indian Songs

THERE is a wide difference among tribes regarding the words of songs. Some tribes use only a few words, occurring usually midway through the song, the remainder of the melody being sung with vocables. Miss Fletcher states that among the Omaha these vocables were distinct syllables, and she transcribes them as *oh, ah* or *ay,* saying that they are never changed. In the writer's experience, the syllables are not always enunciated so clearly; the Indian separates the tones by a peculiar action of his throat muscles. It is impossible to indicate these sounds in spelling, as they are not actual syllables. Many songs have no words, the tones being separated in the manner indicated. Even thirty-second notes can thus be sung by an Indian. The Indians say this is "just *singing.*"

If few words are used they are indicative of an extended idea, being a sort of shorthand or abbreviation. Thus a Chippewa song in honor of a warrior contains only two words, one meaning "warrior" and the other being the man's name—Little Eagle. The people knew his valiant deeds and it was not considered necessary to mention even one of them. A "secret language" is used in songs of religious organizations, so that only the initiate will understand them. In some tribes the songs said to have been received in dreams are in a "dream language," its meaning probably known only to the person who received the song. The words of many songs recorded by the writer are in a form of language not used at the present time. In some instances the meaning is known, as a few words of the obsolete language are still in use, but the Yuma recorded many old songs with continuous words whose meaning they did not know. They said they sang the words exactly as they had been taught by the old men, but the meaning of the words was lost forever.

The Grand Medicine Society (Midewiwin) of the Chippewa uses mnemonics to represent the essential ideas or words in its songs (see page 22). These identify the song to the initiate but are not like our printed page. The mnemonics represent only the key-words in a song, their association conveying the meaning. It is permissible for a member of the society to vary the unimportant words when singing the song, which is often followed by a discourse. The words of these songs are connected with the teachings of the society.

In the songs of some tribes the words are sung without change in the several renditions, while in other tribes some of the songs have many stanzas, the change of words making slight changes in the count-divisions. It is not unusual to find words of two languages in the same song, where tribes using these languages live near together and each understands or perhaps speaks the two languages. The Indians like to "use the words that are easiest to sing," preferring a language that has broad vowel sounds. Thus a majority of the Makah songs are in the language of their neighbors on Vancouver Island, which does not contain so many consonants as their own. They say, for example, that the melody is that of an old Makah song but the words are "B. C.," meaning "British Columbia." New words are frequently sung to an old melody. The name of a recent hero frequently replaces that of an old warrior in a war song, as though we were to substitute the name of Pershing for that of Dewey in one of our songs. This shows the conservatism of Indian musicians and their preference for the old melodies.

In the words of the songs used in treating the sick there are two principal elements, a reference to the source of the doctor's power and an affirmation that the sick person will recover, both being intended to assist the cure. Such a song may mention a spirit bird or animal which, it is believed, gives the doctor his power. A Sioux song used in treating fractures contains the words, "Bear told me to do this," referring to the manner of treatment. Eagle Shield said he sang this song four times while "getting ready to apply the medicine" to a fracture. A Chippewa healing song affirms: "You will recover; you will walk again. It is I who say it; my power is great. Through our white shell I will enable you to walk again." The white shell is the emblem of the Grand Medicine Society and a source of power among its members.

The poetry of the American Indians was embodied in their songs and rituals, and this poetry is frequently of a high order. It is impossible for an interpreter or a white man to supplement the poetic thought of an Indian. The interpreter who translates literally, without paraphrasing or enlarging upon the idea, is the only interpreter whose work is reliable. The words often sound absurd to him, and he is tempted to introduce the phraseology of the missionary, but when this is done the native quality disappears. It is to the credit of our government and mission schools that a conscientious interpreter, working slowly and carefully, can use the English language with rare discrimination. He usually *thinks* a long time and gives the deep sigh which seems to belong especially to Indian interpreters. Perhaps he consults the singer as to the exact meaning of certain words, then he chooses the English equivalents before he begins the translation. When he finally delivers the translation it represents his best effort and is seldom changed. His use of adjectives is discriminating and he does not use qualifying words such as "very" or "most."

Owl Woman, a medicine woman of the Papago, sang this song when she began her treatment of the sick:

> How shall I begin my songs
> In the blue night that is settling?

Can you not see the Arizona night coming swiftly, while in the little adobe hut Owl Woman begins her fight for the life of a sick man? She said that a disembodied spirit came back and gave her a song with these words:

> In the great night my heart will go out,
> Toward me the darkness comes rattling,
> In the great night my heart will go out.

The Yuma and Cocopa Indians also live near the Mexican border and their songs are full of poetry, though very short. Among them are the following:

(1)
The water-bug is drawing the shadows of evening toward
him across the water.

(2)
The owl hooted and told of the morning star,
He hooted again and told of the dawn.

These were part of a long series of dancing songs, the series lasting an entire night. A white person might say, "How can the Indians dance hour after hour, and how monotonous the music sounds!" But the Indians enjoy the words of such songs as we enjoy our own classics, and can hear them only when the dance is in progress.

The friendliness felt by the Indian toward nature is shown in this song, the words being those of one of the "creators":

> I have made you.
> The red evening I give you.

A poetic quality is found also in songs of the north country. Only one who knows the prairie can appreciate the "feeling in the air" which is expressed in this Chippewa song:

> As my eyes search the prairie
> I feel the summer in the spring.

A song of the Acoma [8] contains these words:

There in the west is the home of the rain gods,
There in the west is their water pool,
In the middle of the water pool is the spruce tree that they use as a ladder,
Up from the water pool the rain gods draw the crops which give us life,
East from there, on the place where we dance, they lay the crops,
Then up from that place the people receive crops and life.

From the Makah, living on Cape Flattery, we have this song to a baby boy:

---

[8] This and the Makah song are from unpublished material by the writer, in the possession of the Bureau of American Ethnology.

My little son,
You will put a sealing spear into your canoe without knowing what use you will make of it when you are a man.

The foregoing examples are given in the words of the various interpreters. A multitude of other examples could be presented, showing the beauty and delicacy of Indian poetry in songs and rituals.

Mention should here be made of songs composed in modern times concerning events of current interest. For such songs it is customary to put new words to an old melody. Particularly interesting are the songs composed by Indians while serving with the United States Army, during the World War. Many were recorded among the Winnebago and the Pawnee. A majority were old songs, with words about airplanes or the Germans. There was special mention of the flag and their desire to protect it.

Children's Songs

WE cannot imagine a mother without a lullaby, and the Indian women croon to their babies just as mothers do in our own race. The lullabies were not composed, nor "received in dreams" (like the important songs), but they developed gradually from the gentle crooning sounds with which the mothers soothed the little children. An old Indian smiled when I asked him about lullabies, and said "the women used to sing something to the children," but he did not dignify a lullaby by the name of "song." Sometimes the women record only a sort of "endless tune" when asked for a lullaby, but in many tribes there are distinct melodies sung to the babies. Such a lullaby was found among the Chippewa and their neighbors the Menominee, the same melody with slight variation being recorded in many localities through Minnesota and Wisconsin. The Chippewa woman still swings her baby in a little hammock made of a blanket and sings a lullaby which

No. 5

CHIPPEWA LULLABY [9]

---

[9] *Chippewa Music,* Bulletin 45, Bureau of American Ethnology, No. 145.

CHILDREN'S SONGS

has no words—only the syllable *"way,"* which is part of a word meaning "swinging."

Three lullabies were recorded among the Yuma. One contained only the words, "Sleep, my son [or daughter], sleep." Another imposes a rather heavy burden on the baby, for it says: "Sleep, sleep. It will carry you into the land of wonderful dreams. In those dreams you will see a future day and your future family." The third Yuma lullaby has the words: "What made you cry? Did you step on a thorn?" One can imagine the brown toddler on the desert sand with its prickly plants, and think of the many mothers who have soothed little bare feet.

The customs concerning children are particularly interesting among the Makah, where the presence of servants made it possible for mothers to enjoy the infancy of their children. It was required that everyone be happy and cheerful when near a baby, so that the little one "would not get discouraged and die." Old women came and sang to the baby in its cradle and were rewarded with food. Such songs were usually addressed to the baby or supposedly sung by the child. One of these songs contains the words, "Little baby, how tiny you are." In another song the child is supposed to say, "Because my parents want to trade me for a good-for-nothing little old pot I am going to be a good fisherman." If a child were fretful it was sometimes said to be tired from working too hard. A song for a fretful baby girl contains the words: "My! How I hate to be the older sister of so many boys. My back is sore from packing so much of what they had in their canoes when they came in." Perhaps the most tender of the songs for little children is that of a Mandan mother whose song is freely translated as follows: " 'I want to keep you, little fox,' she said. The little fox said, 'It is not right that you want to keep me.' She said, 'You are my little baby.' "

The Indians encourage a child to dance as soon as it can be held erect, teaching it to lift its little feet with the motion of a dancer. A Mandan song for little children has the words, "Chop your feet, little fox," meaning, "Move your feet sharply up and down, as though you were chopping something." It is interesting to note the term "little fox" applied to the Indian babies with their bright brown eyes, and we remember that the kit-fox was highly regarded by many tribes.

Among the Ute Indians the stories for children are sung to a sort of endless melody. Such songs, phonographically recorded, show no recurrent phrase on an entire cylinder and would seem meaningless except that each song has its own characteristic. The stories are about animals and the melodies have some of the characteristics of the animals. Thus the story of a race between the mice and the tadpoles is in a rapid tempo, while the story of the bear who stole the wolf's wife is a heavier type of melody, in much slower tempo. These are regarded as "rudimentary melodies" and are not analyzed with the Indian songs.

Probably every tribe has its stories for children in which songs are interpolated. It is said that one old woman acted out her stories, dancing and moving around the lodge as the narrative might require. Such stories were usually about animals and were distinct from those related by persons who might be called "professional story tellers" and were paid for their services.

CHILDREN'S SONGS

The children had games of various sorts, with accompanying songs which were short and had few words. In one game the little girls stood behind one another, each girl with her hands on the shoulders of the girl in front of her. They went around the village in a wavering line, singing a song translated, "The deer follow each other." In another game they sat in a circle, and each little girl tickled the hand of the girl next to her until they all rolled over in a state of helpless laughter. The words of the song meant, "I catch but cannot hold you." The children also had games of "pretend" in which they imitated the action of older persons, with appropriate songs.

The "game of silence" was devised by the Chippewa to keep the children quiet in the evening and at the same time teach them to avoid making a sound when surprised. This was very desirable, as a startled child, making an outcry, might endanger the lives of many persons if the enemy were prowling near the village. The song of this game was sung by an older person and the words were an exciting narrative, with frequent change of subject. The length of the song and the quality of the story depended upon the singer and the immediate purpose of the game. It appears that the song generally began with the statement that a very fat pig was up in a tree; then the narrative veered to a fight among "the people who live in a hollow tree" [white people living in log cabins]; and to a rich man carrying a pack on his back. At some unknown point the singer would stop short with the exclamation "Sep!" Any child who made a sound of surprise was out of the game. The child who tood this test the longest received a pile of presents p aced in the middle of the lodge before the game began. Sometimes, if the elders wanted the children to go to sleep so they could discuss important matters, the narrative contained in the song was rather prosy. The singer did not cry "Sep," and the children fell asleep while listening. Usually, however, they were given a chance to show their self-control, and a game that was not decided one evening was renewed the next morning as soon as they awoke. The presents consisted of bows and arrows, belts, moccasins and other articles dear to the hearts of little Indian children.

Songs Belonging to Individuals

THE three general classes of individual songs are (1) songs received in dreams, (2) songs purchased from their owners, and (3) songs praising a man's success or generosity. The first and second classes were believed to have magic power, while the songs of the third class were regarded as an honor and their singing was usually rewarded with gifts. To these may be added the songs inherited in families, a custom prevailing in certain tribes. The rituals, many of which were chanted each year by individuals, are not considered in this classification. The ownership of songs is still respected by the Indians, and the name of the owner is mentioned when a song is recorded. Thus a man may say, "I am going to record my grandfather's song"; or, "This song belonged to a medicine man who died long ago," mentioning the man's name.

The first song received by an individual in a dream was the boy's "vision song." Later in life he might also receive songs in dreams. Every Indian boy, at the age of about twelve years, was expected to fast for several days and watch for the dream or "vision" in which he saw his individual "spirit helper," and usually received a song from that source. In later years, when he wished to receive "spirit help," he sang the song and also performed certain prescribed acts. Sometimes the boy fasted at home, with his face blackened with charcoal; more often he went away and remained alone, night and day, waiting for his vision; while in some tribes the vigil was ceremonial in character. If he succeeded in obtaining a vision he returned home a serious, thoughtful lad, ready to assume the obligations of his dream. If he failed to obtain a vision he was expected to try again. The Menominee custom shows the manner in which the character of an Indian boy was developed. If he returned without a vision his father, a little later, offered him two dishes, one containing charcoal and the other containing food. The boy might take the charcoal and blacken his face as for his first fast, thus signifying his willingness to try again, or he might take the food, signifying that he chose ease and comfort. This happened very rarely, for a man without a vision was regarded either as a failure in will power or as unfortunate in mentality. The "dream" or vision differed in importance according to the temperament of the boy, but in all Indian tribes the life and character of the man had its background and source of power in his childhood vision. Before undertaking this fast he was instructed chiefly by his parents —told what he must do and what he might expect; but after his successful return he went to an old medicine man and, a child no longer, was instructed by the medicine man concerning the new phase of life on which he had entered. In accordance with his dream he became a medicine man, a warrior or a hunter, being confident that he would receive spirit help in one special line of action, and his future training was directed along that course.

The custom of the Sioux was more ceremonial than that of many other tribes. Siyaka [10] (see Frontispiece) described his dream, saying: "I painted my face white

---
[10] Pronounced Sheeya'ka.

SONGS BELONGING TO INDIVIDUALS

and went to a hilltop. At each of the four points of the compass I placed a buffalo robe and some tobacco. These offerings were to show that I desired messages from the directions of the four winds, and was waiting anxiously to hear the voice of some bird or animal speaking to me in a dream. . . . An owl appeared in this part of my dream. Just before daybreak I saw a bright light coming toward me from the east. It was a man. His head was tied up and he held a tomahawk in his hand. He said, 'Follow me,' and in an instant he changed into a crow. In my dream I followed the crow to a village. He entered the largest tent. When he entered the tent he changed into a man again. Opposite the entrance sat a young man painted red, who welcomed me." So the strange dream progressed until the dreamer was taught a song with the words:

> At night may I roam, against the wind may I roam,
> When the owl is hooting may I roam.

> At dawn may I roam, against the winds may I roam,
> When the crow is calling may I roam.

The owl told him to look toward the west whenever he made a petition and it would be granted, and he would have a long life. The fine character of Siyaka as an old man, as well as his record as a warrior, testified to the faithfulness with which he had fulfilled the requirements and followed the guidance of his boyhood dream.

In the Chippewa village at Lac du Flambeau, Wisconsin, there stood, in 1910, many poles, each near the house of an Indian. On the pole was an oblong frame covered with white cloth on which figures of birds or animals had been traced with colored paint. In many instances the figures were almost effaced by the weather. These figures were the symbols of dream songs that had never been sung. If a man's dream concerned war and he received a song in it, he sang the song when in extreme danger, believing it would secure spirit aid for him in this emergency. But if he never went to war and felt that he would never need to sing the song he might display its symbol in this manner. He did not tell the dream, but those who understood the symbolism of the tribe would recognize its character—whether of war or of treating the sick. The bit of cloth beside his door carried this message—"Here lives a man who dreamed a dream and the mysterious strength of his vision is in him, though he has not exerted it." A stranger in the village —one of our own race—asked, "Are those white rags intended to frighten away the evil spirits?" The white man did not know that the tattered banner with its crude drawing was the symbol of a song that never was sung, a song received in a dream and held as its owner's most precious secret.

Mention has been made of songs purchased from the man who received them in a dream. Such songs were usually connected with the treatment of the sick, and the man who bought them received also the knowledge of a material remedy or other treatment which was made effective by the singing of the song. A man might bestow his "dream name" together with his song upon his namesake. The person selling a song does not lose his own use of it but shares the power of the song, receiving a considerable compensation. A father will not teach such a song to his son without compensation.

SONGS BELONGING TO INDIVIDUALS

Tribes differ in the details of the dream custom and the power of its song but the foregoing may be regarded as representative of Indian belief and practice.

The third class of individual songs has been designated as "praise songs," or "honor songs." As indicated in the chapter on "Words of Indian Songs," it was a frequent custom to insert a new name in an old song. This was a compliment, as it implied that a living man had distinguished himself as greatly as a hero of the past. When the singers at the drum began such a song the man was expected to rise and dance alone, and he usually gave a gift to the singers or even distributed gifts to the company. Such songs were often used as a means to secure donations, the song praising a man or a member of his family in such a manner that he could not refuse the call. A Sioux song in honor of Two Bears contained the words, "The tribe, whenever they council, Two Bears never refuses." Another song, praising Two White Buffalo, is as follows: "Two White Buffalo, take courage, the committee depend upon you, they said, hence the white metal (money) you donated." Could Two Bears or Two White Buffalo fail to live up to such a reputation?

A noble memorial to a slain warrior is contained in a Sioux song in honor of Sitting Crow, the words being, "Sitting Crow, that is the way he wished to lie; he is lying as he desired." A Chippewa scalp dance song in honor of a warrior who brought home a scalp contained the words, "Ojibwa brings back our brother." The war party had gone to avenge the death of a member of the tribe and it was considered that Ojibwa, in bringing an enemy's scalp and presenting it to a sister of the dead man, had "restored" her brother.

An excellent example of a song belonging to an individual is a song of Sitting Bull. He appears to have had several songs but this is of peculiar interest. In explanation it was said: "The last time that Sitting Bull was in a regular tribal camp was in the year 1889. The Sioux were camped together on the Standing Rock reservation to consider ceding some land. Sitting Bull used to go around the camp circle every evening just before sunset on his favorite horse, singing this song" (No. 6).

It has been stated that a man rose and danced when the singers at the drum started his individual song. There were also circumstances under which a man rose and sang his own song. For example, at a Pawnee gathering held to celebrate the return of Pawnee soldiers from the World War, the older men, in their joy, rose and sang their own songs, sometimes two or three being on their feet at the same time, singing and rejoicing.

In the customs pertaining to individual songs, more than in many other phases of this subject, we note the difference between the Indian beliefs and practices and our own.

SONGS BELONGING TO INDIVIDUALS

No. 6
SIOUX SONG BELONGING TO SITTING BULL [11]

The tribe named me, so in courage I shall live,
It is reported Sitting Bull said this.

---

[11] *Teton Sioux Music,* Bulletin 61, Bureau of American Ethnology, No. 194.

[85]

Love Songs

IT is probable that the world would not have reached its present interest in Indian music if our artists had not sung Indian love songs, and yet the writer has been repeatedly informed that songs concerning the passion of love were not sung by the old-time Indians except in the working of "love charms." There are many love songs on Indian reservations at the present time but they are modern and do not represent a phase of life which is creditable to the Indians. These are considered later in this chapter. The only Indian tribe which appeared to have used songs expressing admiration for persons of the opposite sex is the Makah, living at the end of Cape Flattery. As noted, the position of women is different among tribes of the northwest coast, where the caste system prevailed, from what it is, for example, among the Plains tribes, where women shared the manual work with the men of the tribe.

In the absence of love songs among the old-time Indians we see an evidence of their delicacy and sensitiveness as well as their silence concerning whatever was deepest and most sacred in their feelings. The Indian knew how to leave a great deal unsaid, and he trusted more to silence than we, in our day of "much talking."

Mention has been made of the use of songs in working magic and attracting a person of the opposite sex. This custom does not seem to have prevailed in all tribes and was not favorably regarded. Such a song, accompanied by the use of some "charm," was gener-

LOVE SONGS

ally used for an evil purpose and has nothing to do with the love song of the present time. My Papago interpreter said: "Love songs are dangerous. If a man gets to singing them we send for a medicine man to treat him and make him stop." In all the tribes visited I find it necessary to apologize for an interest in love songs, explaining that only a few are wanted, in order that all classes of songs may be represented in my work. The old Indians say they were not sung in the old days. The Sioux said their nearest approach to love songs consisted of a very few concerning a man's qualification to support a wife—whether he had enough ponies or had been successful on the warpath. Such a song was recorded by Two Shields, one of the most reliable old singers on the Standing Rock reservation in North and South Dakota. The words are in the Sioux language (No. 7).

A Pawnee chief, John Luwak, said that his people had a few old songs in which people who had been married a long time expressed a hope that if one died the other would "cry" and would not marry too soon, but he declared that the modern love song arose among a "low class" of Pawnee who lived near towns and worked for the white people. Among the Chippewa and Menominee it is said that love songs are modern and are usually associated with disappointment or intoxication. The development of the modern love song appears to have been greatest in tribes living in close contact with the fringes of civilization.

The playing of a flute at dusk was a general custom in all tribes. Young boys did it at the bashful age, and young men did it when really in love. Perhaps the first form of love song (apart from those used in "magic")

No. 7
YOU MAY GO ON THE WARPATH (SIOUX) [12]

Ho-we zu-ya ya - ye ho-we zu-ya ya - ye

ho-we zu-ya ya - ye to-kśa ća - że na-ći-hoŋ kiŋ-haŋ hiŋ-gna

ci-yin kte

A is pronounced as in *father*, E as in *they*, and I as in *marine;* C has the sound of *ch* in *chin*, S has the sound of *sh* in *shall*, Z has the sound of *s* in *pleasure*, and N is pronounced like *n* in *drink;* other letters have the same sounds as in English.

(Translation)

You may go on the warpath,
When your name I hear [announced among the victors]
Then I will marry you.

consisted of an imitation of a flute melody, sung instead of played in order that words might be added to the melody. Thus the Indian emerged a little from his native reticence and used words in his musical lovemaking. I have recorded such songs and they resemble the melodies played on the flute, but in these, as well as in the modern love songs, it is wise not to ask a literal

---

[12] *Teton Sioux Music*, Bulletin 61, Bureau of American Ethnology, No. 151.

translation. It appears that the young girls, as well as the boys, had a courting call. An old Yuma said: "Sometimes the girls hid in the bushes, two or three together, and played the jews-harp to attract the boys. You just could not get by if you went that way." From this it is evident that youth is the same in every race, but we must bear in mind that marriages among the Indians were usually arranged by the parents, in the old days, and were restricted to certain groups which were believed not to have a blood relationship to one another.

It is admitted that there are many love songs on Indian reservations at the present time. They are plaintive melodies and some of them approach more nearly to our idea of Indian music than the genuine old melodies of the race. On one occasion, when collecting songs on the Standing Rock reservation, I strolled far out on the prairie at evening and, returning, heard some delightful songs emanating from the guardhouse —wild, sweet, haunting melodies coming through those barred windows in the twilight. The next day I said to Robert P. Higheagle, my interpreter, "Why do you not get me some beautiful songs such as I heard last evening when passing the guardhouse?" He replied: "Those were love songs. The men were put in there because they had been drinking. If you recorded those songs the old chiefs such as John Grass would have nothing more to do with our work." The Chippewa use a peculiar nasal drawl when singing their love songs. This tone is not used in any other class of songs and at times resembles a *yowl,* as it rises and falls in slow, sliding cadences. Among the Chippewa and Menominee the words of most of the love songs are forlorn, expressing disappointment rather than affection. There are also taunting songs and others concerning harsh words and quarrels. All this is in strong contrast to the quiet dignity and poetry of the old songs.

The following are typical of the words of modern Chippewa love songs:

(1)
I sit here thinking of her;
I am sad as I think of her.

(2)
Come, I beseech you, let us sing,
Why are you offended?

(3)
I do not care for you any more;
Someone else is in my thoughts.

(4)
You desire vainly that I seek you,
The reason is, I come to see your younger sister.

(5)
Come, let us drink.

The three next following are from the Menominee.

(1)
At some future time you will think of me and cry,
My sweetheart.

(2)
You had better go home,
Your mother loves you so much.

(3)
O my! How that girl loves me—
The one I am secretly courting.

LOVE SONGS

An interesting Indian love song was recorded by Mrs. Mary Warren English, a member of the Chippewa tribe and a sister of William Warren, historian of the Chippewa. Mrs. English died in 1926, at the age of about ninety-one, and this song belongs to the time of her girlhood on Madeline Island. It has some of the characteristics of the modern love song but is of a higher standard.

No. 8
CHIPPEWA LOVE SONG (With Chippewa Words) [13]

[13] *Chippewa Music,* Bulletin 45, Bureau of American Ethnology, No. 135.

A is pronounced as in *father*, E as in *they*, and I as in *marine*; G as in *get*, and S as in *sin*; C is pronounced like *sh*, and ŋ is like *ng*. Short I and E have the accustomed sounds and û is pronounced as in *but*. U, unmarked, is pronounced as in *rule*.

(*Translation*)

A loon I thought it was,
But it was my love's splashing oar.
To Sault Ste. Marie he has departed,
My love has gone on before me,
Never again can I see him.
A loon I thought it was,
But it was my love's splashing oar.

Musical Instruments

THE American Indians had two types of musical instruments—wind and percussion. The former comprised flutes and whistles, and the latter included drums and various sorts of rattles. So far as noted, the Tule Indians of Panama (commonly called the "white Indians") are the only Indians who do not use a drum nor pound upon anything, their only instrument of percussion being a gourd rattle. The Apache is believed to be the only tribe that has used a stringed instrument. The Mexicans usually carry a violin and play it with their dances, and the "Apache fiddle" was probably adapted from that source. It has only one or two strings, the body is shorter than that of a violin and cylindrical in shape, and one end is pressed against the player's abdomen when it is played. The bow is short, with a curved stick. Examples of this instrument are in the United States National Museum at Washington.

In making his musical instruments, the Indian used the materials he had at hand, ornamenting them with symbolic designs or in a manner that pleased his fancy. The materials varied with the environment of the tribes and included wood, bone, hides, gourds, cane (often called bamboo), turtle and cocoanut shells, deer hoofs, the quills of large birds, pebbles and pottery, as well as shot, pitch, sinew, bark and glue. To these may be added the materials used in making the baskets which the southern tribes use as drums, while the Yaqui use the intestines of cattle as a wrapping for flutes. Greasewood and the rib of the sahauro cactus also furnish material for making musical instruments. The woods most commonly used in the making of musical instruments are cedar, ash, box-elder, sumac and hickory, while hazel, grapevine and willow are used for making drumsticks.

Among the decorative materials are feathers, native paint, strips of hide in fringes or tassels, fur, beads, bright cloth or yarn, the heads and necks of birds, and little "bells" or "jingles" made of bits of tin. Further decoration is sometimes obtained by etching the wood with a heated iron, tracing lines which are left brown from the searing of the wood or filled with native paint.

Wind Instruments

THE two wind instruments used by the Indians are the flute and whistle, the former having fingerholes by which the pitch of the tone is varied. If the whistle is sufficiently long, it is possible for the player to produce part of the harmonic series by "overblowing," as on a bugle. The flute and long whistle were chiefly played by young men to please the maidens; and the short whistle was used chiefly by magicians when giving exhibitions of their power, by doctors when treating the sick, by warriors and in war societies, and in certain ceremonies, notably by men taking part in the Sioux Sun dance. It is interesting to note that the flute was sometimes used as a war signal, a man playing it around the village in a manner understood as a warning to the people, while the enemy supposed it to be a young man playing to his sweetheart.

The typical Indian flute is a true flute-a-bec, played by blowing into an air chamber in the upper end, the sound being produced by a whistle-mouthpiece similar to that of an organ pipe. The variation of pitch in the tones is produced by the manipulation of fingerholes in the body of the instrument. Such flutes are made of various kinds of soft, straight-grained wood, like cedar and sumac. A straight, round stick of the wood is split lengthwise into two equal parts. Each half-cylinder is then hollowed out, except near one end, where a bridge is left, so that when the two pieces are put together there is formed a cylindrical tube open at both ends and throughout its length except at one point where the bridges form a solid stopper, dividing the tube into a short upper portion (the wind chamber) and a long lower portion (the flute tube). The organ-pipe mouthpiece is ingeniously formed as follows: A square opening is cut through the side of the tube just above the bridge, into the wind chamber, and another is cut below the bridge, into the sounding tube. A block is so fashioned and slightly cut away on its lower surface that it covers the upper opening and directs the air in a thin sheet downward against the lower, sound-producing edge of the square hole below the bridge. To make this edge of the hole smooth and sharp—that is, to form a suitable "lip" for the pipe—a piece of very thin birch bark or other substance such as sheet lead or iron is placed between the tube and the block. The junction between the birch bark and the tube is sometimes made air-tight by a "gasket" of silk cloth; often the joint is closed by resin or other cement. When the flute is completed, the joints along its length are sealed with resin or glue and the parts are held together by several windings of thong or other material. The block is held firmly in position by a winding of thong. The tone of the flute is influenced by the position of the block; sometimes this is sealed in its most effective position and sometimes it is held only by the winding, so that it can be adjusted by the player. The fingerholes are from four to six in number and are sometimes equidistant throughout and sometimes arranged in two groups, each hole in the group being equidistant from the others. The late Charles Kasson Wead, for many years an examiner of patents in the United States Patent Office and author of several treatises on the physics of music, appears to have been the first to suggest that the spacing of the fingerholes on an Indian flute was a matter of esthetics and that the resultant tones were not a pre-determined scale. Indians in all tribes questioned by the writer say that the fingerholes in a flute are spaced in a manner convenient to the player's hand, not by any fixed rule. Some flutes have a row of holes around the lower end which resemble those on Chinese flutes and have no musical purpose. The length of a typical Indian flute varies with the stature of the player, a desirable length being from the inside of the elbow to the end of the middle-finger. Melodies played on such a flute have been phonographically recorded by the writer in several tribes, and the results transcribed as nearly as possible in musical notation. The northern Ute Indians use a flute only about eleven inches long, with six fingerholes arranged in two groups, the holes within each group being equidistant.

Flutes are sometimes made from a stick of box-elder from which the pith has been entirely removed. These are simple open pipes in which the sound is produced by blowing across the open end, the edge of the tube forming the "lip" or embouchure.

Pottery flutes were used by the Zuni, and flutes made of gun barrels are not uncommon among the Plains tribes.

The Indians of southern Arizona, having no wood, make their flutes of cane, which, as has been said, is commonly called bamboo. A joint of the cane corresponds to the bridge in the wooden flute, and in the simplest form of this flute the player's finger is held above the opening in place of the block. In other flutes a strip of paper is tied around the flute and adjusted,

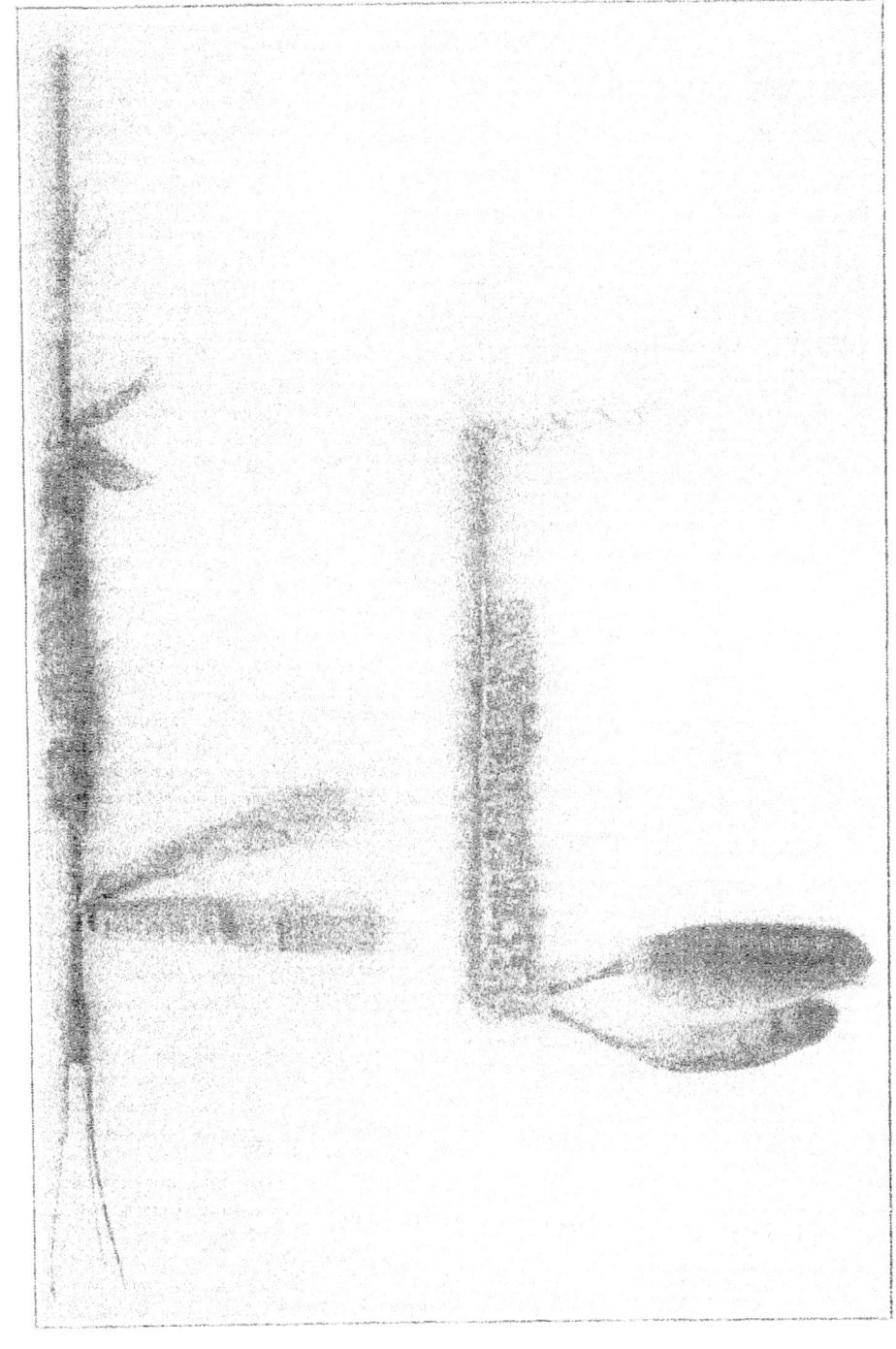

ILLUSTRATION 2.—COURTING WHISTLE AND DANCE RATTLE

WIND INSTRUMENTS

like the block, to direct the current of air. A transverse flute of cane was obtained by the writer from a Yuma Indian. Legends of the origin of the flute appear in the mythology of many tribes, showing the use of the flute to be very old. An old Indian said: "There has always been a flute, just as there have always been young people. The flute is as old as the world."

Mention may here be made of a unique cane flute collected by the writer when studying the music of the Seminole in Florida. The removal of the septums is the same as in all cane flutes but the detached piece which forms the "whistle-head" is flush with the tube instead of being in the form of a block above the tube. It is tied in place with a buckskin thong, as in the wooden flutes with a block. This flute has four fingerholes spaced in about the usual manner, and has also two holes bored transversely through the cane at right angles to the sound holes.

Whistles vary in length from the small whistle made of the wingbone of a bird to the long wooden whistle used as a "courting call" and in certain dances. Double whistles like pan-pipes were formerly used by the Mandan and were made of quills of very large birds, varying in length and fastened side by side.

Two types of courting whistles were used among the Mandan and Hidatsa at Fort Berthold. The first type had the open end carved to represent the head of a bird (Illustration 2, A) resembling in this respect the Grass dance whistle of the Sioux and other tribes. The second type was said to be like this except that the end was not carved. This was called an "elk whistle" and was said to have originated in a dream. A certain man

AMERICAN INDIANS AND THEIR MUSIC

saw an elk in his dream and the elk gave him one of these whistles, telling him to use it in courting. The length of this whistle depended upon the stature of the man who was to use it, the usual measurement being from the tips of the fingers of the right hand, along the right arm, across the chest and to the shoulder joint of the left arm. It does not appear that the first type of whistle was so long as this, the instrument illustrated being only twenty-two and five-eighths inches below the mouth. In construction it is an open pipe, with the usual whistle mouthpiece. The range of this instrument (phonographically recorded) was from D flat, fourth line treble staff, upward for ten tones, the instrument producing tones of the long harmonic series, within that compass.

A whistle without decoration was used by medicine men. If such a man were on his way to treat a sick person he usually had his whistle fastened to the band of his hat. The Sun dance whistle was solidly covered with a braiding of porcupine quills, and tipped with a downy eagle feather, while the mouthpiece was covered with fresh sage. As the man danced, he blew this whistle and the filaments of the downy feather were moved gently by his breath. The whistle used in certain societies of warriors was covered with beads.

The ceremonial use of a whistle is described by Miss Fletcher in *The Hako: A Pawnee Ceremony*. In connection with a ritual song it is said "the whistle was used as the white eagle whistled when he flew around his nest." A similar whistle was used in the Wa-wan ceremony of the Omaha, and constituted one of the ceremonial articles. The "frog-whistle of the frog-dancer and the whistle of the fire-dancer," as well as other whistles of the Kwakiutl, are mentioned by Dr. Franz Boas in his writings on this tribe. Reed instruments, commonly called whistles, are used by Indians on the northwest coast.

Drums

THE three general types of drums used by the Indians are (1) the hand drum, (2) the large drum around which several men are seated, and (3) the "water drum" which resembles a keg and is partly filled with water when in use. Other forms of percussion instruments are a pole or a plank beside which the players are seated, pounding with short sticks, and a stiff rawhide held by a circle of players who beat it with a stick with one hand while holding it with the other. In this way the rawhide is often carried around the camp by "begging-parties." Certain tribes of the northwest coast use a long box as a drum. This is "played" by men who sit on it and kick their heels against it. In southern Arizona the writer saw halves of gourds used in the manner of small drums by the Yaqui. One of the half-gourds was inverted on the water in a tub and the other placed on the ground, both being struck with short sticks as accompaniment to the Deer dance. On the southern desert, where hides are scarce and basket-making material abundant, the Indians invert a household basket on the ground and use it as a drum, striking it with the palms of the hands, with sticks or with bundles of arrow-weed. Two sticks may be struck together, or a song may be accompanied by the stamping of feet or the clapping of hands.

The hand drum varies in size and may have one or two heads. Probably the drum with one head is used by the greater number of tribes. It requires less material for the head, which is an advantage in many localities, and it is held more easily. A single-headed drum is carried by a "hand-hold" at the back (see Illustration 1) and can be used by a man when standing, walking, riding or dancing, while a double-headed drum is held by a loop on one edge and usually rests against the knee of the player, who is seated. The latter type is used in connection with the moccasin game, the players being seated on the ground. Sometimes these drums have "snares" consisting of pegs fastened to cords that are stretched across the inside of the drumhead in such a manner as to vibrate against it when the drum is struck.

The paint on a drum may be decorative or symbolic. Drums of the Plains tribe frequently show pictures of tipis or buffalo, while a very large drum from the northwest coast is decorated with drawings of whales and ships. A Chippewa war drum shows a drawing of the lightning and a turtle. The owner of the drum said the lightning was a picture of his dream and the sound of his drum was like the rumble of thunder. He said that he added the turtle because it was always supposed to be such a good warrior. He carried this drum when fighting the Sioux, and when the hide needed renewing he duplicated the design on the new cover.

In some of the single-headed hand drums the corners of the hide which forms the head are tied together to form a hand-hold on the reverse side, but more frequently the hide is fastened to the hoop and the hand-hold is formed by two wires, thongs or strips of cloth. These cross the back of the hoop at right angles and there is some sort of short bar at their intersection by which the drum can conveniently be held. A drum of this sort was often used by an individual when singing alone. A Sioux medicine man, for example, used such a drum with his healing songs, and a Makah woman declined to sell her hand drum, saying it was "so much company in the long winter evenings," when she sang by herself. When hand drums are used in a large gathering it is necessary to have several of them, and the Indians say they "like those that tune together." Thus in certain dances of the Ute there were usually four men with hand drums who stood in a row, and behind them stood a row of singers, while the dancers moved in front of them. Drums of this sort were also carried by men on horseback, in parades around the camp circle.

The Chippewa, in old times, made a large war drum by placing stakes upright in the ground and stretching a hide over them. In recent years a wooden or metal washtub forms the shell of the large drum used in many tribes as an accompaniment to dancing. A hide is stretched over the top and cloth conceals the sides. Sometimes an ordinary bass drum is used in a similar manner, and the decoration is omitted. In common usage, a drum of this type is placed flat on the ground and the players sit around it, sometimes eight to ten in number, each pounding it with his stick and singing. In ceremonial usage, however, the drum is suspended from curved stakes so that it hangs a few inches above the ground (Illustration 3). This is the custom among the Menominee and neighboring Chippewa, the drum having a religious significance and its decorations being symbolic.

A water drum is made of a log and partly filled with water when in use. This increases its resonance so that a drum of this sort can be heard a long distance; one

DRUMS

ILLUSTRATION 3—LARGE DECORATED DRUM

has been heard twelve miles across a lake. The drum is made by burning a log (usually basswood) and scraping away the charred portion until a cylinder is formed. Into one end of this a wooden disc is fitted, and about halfway up the side a small hole is drilled with a hot iron and stopped with a wooden plug. Through this hole the water can be emptied from the drum. The deer hide used for the top of this drum is usually allowed to dry hard. It is moistened when laid over the opening and held down by a hoop wound with cloth.

This hoop fits snugly against the side of the drum and holds the hide in place so that it dries evenly. If the hide becomes too dry the drummer may moisten his hand and pass it over the hide or he may "splash" the hide with the water inside the drum. If in doing this he moistens the hide too much, he will tighten it by placing it in the sun for a short time. A typical water drum is about sixteen and one-half inches high, ten inches in diameter at the base and eight and one-half inches across at the top. Among the Chippewa and Menominee, who use this drum in the Medicine ceremony, it is decorated in a symbolic manner, frequently showing the "spirits," or the degree in the Medicine Society attained by its owner. Miss Fletcher states that a similar drum is used ceremonially by the Pawnee and the Omaha.

The drum used in the peyote organization (Native American Church) consists of a kettle with a top of animal hide held in place by an ingenious contrivance used on no other drum. Instead of the usual hoop, this drum has a number of marbles or small stones placed beneath the portion of the hide that falls over the side of the drum. These are connected by a heavy cord, making possible the tightening of the top. The details of the contrivance are too long for present consideration. The kettle is partly filled with water.

The rhythm of the drum-beat varies with the character of the song which it accompanies. Generally speaking, the songs connected with medicine practices or ceremonials are accompanied by drum-beats in eighth notes (two beats to each quarter-note of the melody), either unaccented or accented in groups of two. In dance and game songs the accented beat is often preceded by an unaccented stroke of shorter duration; this, in turn, preceded by a short rest. Thus the drum-beat in such songs frequently has an unaccented stroke corresponding approximately to the last note of a triplet, with the second note as a rest; and sometimes resembling the last note in a group of four, the first in each group being strongly accented. Occasionally the short, unaccented stroke seems to follow the accented, like a rebound. Instances of elaborate drumming are not unusual in music phonographically recorded by the writer, the changes in the regular drum-beat taking place at the same point in every rendition of a song. There are also individual peculiarities of drumming, constituting a sort of virtuosity that is indulged in by expert drummers.

In the earlier study of Indian music there was much comment on the "two-against-three" rhythm, referring to a combination of two drum-beats with three melody tones, or vice versa, and the statement was made that Indians can do with ease what white musicians do only with difficulty. In this, as in too many respects, the white man seems anxious to be inferior to the Indian without studying into the matter. The cumulative evidence of the writer's analysis of Indian songs is that Indians are able to carry two rhythms (meters) simultaneously, one with the voice and the other with the drum, a coincidence being accidental, though there are, of course, many songs in which the rhythms of voice and drum are identical. Our understanding of the "two-against-three" rhythm is a unit of time divided into two parts by one medium of expression and into three by another. When the Indian has a double rhythm in one part of his music and a triple in the other it is the writer's opinion that he actually thinks each rhythm separately, caring little whether the unit of group-measurement is the same in the two parts. In many Chippewa songs the tempo of the drum is $\dot{\TextOrMath{\quarternote}{}}=100$ and that of the voice is $\quarternote=112$, each tempo being steadily maintained, though drum and voice seldom synchronize. This is *horizontal* music, while harmonized music has been called *perpendicular* music. Indian tribes differ in the synchronizing of voice and drum, as in many other respects, but an independence of the two parts is in accord with the individuality and independence of the old native life.

Drumsticks

THE importance attached to the drumstick in certain tribes is one of the differences between the Indian race and our own. There were drumsticks made for utility and others which were highly decorated, but the drumstick peculiar to the Indian is that with a symbolic meaning, used in ceremonies. The ordinary drumstick consisted of a straight stick with a padded end, usually formed by a winding of rags. The stick might be of grapevine, hazel, or any wood having the desired resilience. Such sticks were quickly made and were often discarded after being used at a dance. The leader of the drummers, however, might have a drumstick covered with soft leather decorated with porcupine quills. Sometimes four leading drummers used decorated sticks. This marked them as leaders among the men seated at the drum.

An interesting example of a ceremonial drumstick was obtained among the Mandan and was a replica of that used in the Goose Women Society, long ago. This society was composed of women who held a ceremony every spring and sang songs to benefit the crop of corn. The drum used with these songs was decorated with goose-tracks, placed close together on the rawhide head, near the edge. The stick symbolized an ear of corn. The wood at the end was scraped and turned downward, the inner bark being left in narrow strips, between which were twelve spaces. Thus it resembled a twelve-row ear of corn with the silk turned downward. Soft eagle feathers were placed over this, and the cover was of buffalo hide fastened with a strip of the same material.

The Chippewa attached much importance to the drumsticks used with songs of the Grand Medicine Society (Midewiwin). They often replaced a water drum but continued to use the same stick. The shape of all these sticks was the same, consisting of a rather slender stick, perhaps thirteen to sixteen inches long, turned sharply downward at the end which struck the drum, but this end was carved in various forms. A very old drumstick was obtained from a member of the Midewiwin, who said the carved end represented the head of a loon, and that "the members of the Grand Medicine stretch their hands toward the western ocean, where the loon rises from the water and gives a signal, showing that he responds to their call." The entire concept of the Grand Medicine is connected with water, the animals that dwell in it, and the birds that fly above it.

Among the Menominee of Wisconsin a Drum ceremony was seen. This may be regarded as one form of the messiah cult and originated with the Sioux. During the ceremony a drum was presented by the Chippewa to the Menominee, and at a certain point in the ceremony there was used a drumstick more than three feet long. The skin from the neck of a loon was slipped over the curved end of the drumstick, its glossy black feathers beautifully dotted with white.

The tribes of southern Arizona who use a basket as a drum have their own peculiar sorts of drumsticks. The Yuma use round willow sticks about an inch in diameter and twelve inches in length, two being held in the player's right hand and used together, never singly.

These are used with certain classes of songs, while with others the singer uses two bundles of arrow-weed, eighteen inches or more in length and perhaps an inch and a half in thickness at the place where they are tied together. These are straight, stiff weeds that grow abundantly in the region and are used for many purposes. The Papago strike the basket usually with the palm of the hand. One or two players may use both hands, but if several are playing there is room for only the right hands on the basket. With certain songs the basket is struck a glancing blow with a short, flat stick.

An instance is recorded in which wooden clappers were used as drumsticks. This was among the Delaware Indians and the drumsticks were flat, "the broader ends cut in prongs, each ornamented with a rudely carved head, one representing the female and the other the male element." A drum, with these clappers, was used in an annual ceremony.

Rattles

ALL tribes of Indians have some form of rattle except certain groups of Eskimo, and even in that region the absence of a rattle is not universal, as there are Eskimo who use a rattle to entice seals into the water. When an Indian of the Plains tribes is using the sign language and wishes to mention a rattle he makes a sign that means "sacred." This sign is the basis of all signs that refer to sacred things. Dr. J. R. Swanton states that in former times the rattle "was generally regarded as a sacred object not to be brought forth on ordinary occasions but confined to rituals, religious feasts, shamanistic performances, etc." The last included the treatment of the sick as well as exhibitions of jugglery. In this connection it is interesting to note that the rattle is essentially a rhythmic instrument and that rhythm is always associated, by Indians, with the supernatural. The drum is also a rhythmic instrument but it lacks the *rebound* of the rattle.

There are three classes of rattles in use among the Indians. First, there is a receptacle containing small objects that produce a sound by hitting together; second, an instrument consisting of objects suspended so that they clash together; third, the notched stick rattle or "rasping stick" used in the southwest. To this may be added the wooden clappers used on the northwest coast. The material used in all rattles is that available to the tribe, and the decorations placed upon them represent the best skill of the people, whether fanciful or symbolic.

The simplest and most widely distributed example of the first type of rattle is that made of a gourd containing small pellets of clay, small stones or shot. The gourd is hollowed out and pierced by a stick that forms the handle. Such gourds are often painted red and occasionally decorated with symbolic designs. A cocoanut shell is similarly used by the Seminole in Florida. Northern tribes make a receptacle of rawhide, pressed into shape and decorated. This is usually flattened in one circumference, not globe-shaped like the gourd. Examples of this type are the Grass dance rattle of the Mandan, which is bordered with eagle feathers, and the Strong Heart Society rattle of the Sioux, bordered with fur. The Northern Woodland tribes make a cylindrical box of heavy birch bark fastened with tiny wooden pegs. This box contains a few pebbles or shot and is pierced by a stick which forms the handle. A tin spice-box often serves the same purpose. Another form of these rattles resembles a very thin, small drum with a few shot in it. Such a rattle is either held in the hand and shaken, or, still smaller in size, is at the end of a stick which forms a handle. The Indians distinguish between the tones of various rattles and like to hear several together, like the drums that "chord together." The rattle last described is one of a set of four Midewiwin rattles obtained from the Chippewa, the others being cylindrical boxes of birch bark and no two having the same tone. This difference of tone is due to the size and number of pebbles or shot contained in the rattle. Similarly, a member of the Yuma tribe said that in the Human Being dance from six to ten men sit in a row on a bench and shake the spice-box rattles, the leading singer sitting in the middle of the row and having the loudest rattle. This was not the largest spice-box but the one containing the most shot.

We must go to the northwest coast to find the most elaborate rattles of this type. They are carved of wood and are used chiefly by medicine men. Sometimes the carving is of the character seen on totem poles, one figure merging into another. A curious rattle of the Tlingit is of wood carved in the figure of a bird. Above the head of the bird is a human face with the tongue protruding, and the end of the tongue touches the tongue of a frog. This is said to indicate that the medicine man who owns the rattle absorbs from a frog the poison with which he can work evil upon the people. The decorated rattles of this region present a bewildering variety. Some are in the form of a bird about fourteen inches long, the tail of the bird forming the handle of the rattle; others have two human faces carved on the two sides of the rattle, one sad and the other smiling.

Rattles of this first type are not always held in the hand; they are often fastened to the dancer's leg below the knee. In a Yaqui Deer dance, near Phoenix, Arizona, the leading dancer wore around his right knee a band of cloth to which were attached more than a hundred cocoons sewn together side by side, forming a strip six or eight feet long. Each cocoon contained a few small pebbles that rattled as he danced. This rattle was very old and highly valued by its owner. The shell of a tortoise was used in a similar manner as well as shaken in the hand. The open side of the shell was covered with rawhide, forming a receptacle in which pebbles or shot were placed.

The second class of rattle consists of objects suspended in such a manner that they clash together. Like the first, these may be held in the hand or attached to the body. The materials used in making these rattles are of great variety and include the dew-claws (false hoofs) of the deer, pieces of deer hoof, birds' beaks, elk teeth, pods, shells and dried buffalo tails. A Dog Society rattle (Illustration 2, B) was obtained from Wounded Face, a prominent Mandan living on the Fort Berthold reservation in North Dakota. He said it was held in the dancer's right hand, which hung at his side, the rattle being shaken in that position. Wounded Face recorded an interesting war song with the accompaniment of this rattle. Like many other Indian rattles, it is made of pieces of deer hoof hung on a stick which is wrapped with deerskin. The hoof is boiled to make it tender, after which it is cut in pieces of a triangular shape. A hole is bored in one corner, and through this a string is passed for suspending the piece, this suspension being free enough to permit the bits of hoof to strike against one another when the rattle is shaken.

Several turtle shells are tied around the knee by woman dancers of the Seminole. These do not sound as the women walk to the dance, but rattle with the motion of their dancing.

Copper "tinklers" were used by southwestern tribes, and people of the plains still make the little cones of tin which jingle together. Rattles made of shells have been found in ancient ruins on the Little Colorado River and are still used with sacred songs by Pueblo Indians. An interesting shell rattle was obtained from the Makah, the rattle consisting of four pairs of scallop shells strung on a hoop of thin whalebone and tied with shredded cedar bark. It was used in the treatment of the sick. A graceful rattle used by the Sioux is made of the dew-claws of the deer, attached to a stick, with one or two little strips of soft brown hide in the center of each dew-claw, like the stamens of a little trumpet-shaped flower. The rattle suggests a stem of lilies-of-the-valley or similar flowers. A more somber rattle made of dew-claws was used in a cremation ceremony witnessed among the Yuma Indians in 1922. It consisted of a string or bunch of dew-claws and was said to be two hundred and fifty years old. The leader of the ceremony held it in his hand as one would hold a short string of heavy beads, and shook it ceremonially above the dead body. This rattle served as a record as well as a ceremonial article, one dew-claw having been added for each cremation, until recent times, when it became too difficult to obtain deer in that region.

In this group should be included the wooden clappers used by Indians on the northwest coast. These are of two types, one of which consists of a short thick paddle split lengthwise and having one of the prongs hinged to the handle, while the other consists of two spoon-shaped pieces of wood fastened together with the concave sides facing each other. The former is from the Tlingit and the latter from the Bellabella Indians. It is said that the latter was used by medicine men, who struck it against the body of the patient.

The third class is the notched stick rattle, which consists of two units, a stick (or other substance) having notches cut horizontally across its surface, and a shorter stick (or other substance) that is rubbed perpendicularly across these notches. A resonator is generally used to amplify the sound. A typical instrument consists of a stick about one inch in diameter and twenty to twenty-five inches long, cut with notches on one side for about two-thirds of its length, and rasped with a stick varying in length from six to twelve inches, or with a stout bone. Resonators vary with the locality and will be described later in this section.

The history of this instrument is particularly interesting. The earliest example, so far as known, is the Chinese *ÿu* which was used in the Confucian ceremonies and occupied a position of prominence on the west side of the temple. It was of carved wood in the shape of a crouching tiger on whose back were twenty-seven teeth resembling those of a saw. At the close of each verse in the temple songs, the head of the tiger was struck three times with a split bamboo, which was then passed rapidly over the projections on its back. A similar instrument was used in Japan. Indians on the Amazon use a notched bamboo, and the natives of Java have a carved wooden bird with a bronze plate on its back, scored with deep notches. Evidence of the use of human bones in the making of this instrument have been unearthed in Mexico. The instrument is widely used in the West Indies and in Africa. Bones of animals are used for both parts of the rattle. In Mexico the metatarsal bone of a deer was notched and rubbed with a deer's scapula, while one observer in the United States reports an instrument made of a buffalo rib with notches cut in it. The jaw of a horse or mule with the teeth in it has been similarly used.

The Ute Indians use an instrument of this sort as an accompaniment to the Bear dance, calling it by the Spanish term *morache*. In a typical example the notched stick is shaped like the jawbone of a bear, the

ILLUSTRATION 1—UTE INDIAN WITH NOTCHED STICK RATTLE

ridges between the notches representing the teeth of the animal. This is rubbed or rasped with a bone of a bear, and the sound is said to resemble the growling of a bear. For a resonator the Ute dig a long trench and cover it with sheets of zinc on which they rest the ends of their notched sticks. The trench is said to represent the bear's cave, and the sound of a large number of these instruments as played in the Bear dance can well be imagined. If a dancer fell from exhaustion or by a misstep, the singing ceased and a medicine man came forward to "restore" the dancer. Taking a morache from one of the singers he placed the lower end of the notched stick against the prostrate man's body and passed the rubbing stick rapidly across it; then held the notched stick toward the sky and passed the rubbing stick upward as though he were brushing something into the air. The instrument illustrated is played by Pagits, a Ute medicine man, the notched stick resting on a basket resonator (Illustration 4). This basket is flat and shallow, and is used for no other purpose.

This instrument is used by the Pima in ceremonies to bring rain and is considered so important that the sticks are called "rain sticks." The Papago used the notched stick rattle in treating the sick and also with the songs of expeditions to obtain salt. On these expeditions the Papago visited certain salt deposits near the Gulf of California and the entire procedure was of religious character. Two sets of these sticks were obtained among the Papago and were slender, the notched sticks curved and the rubbing sticks being straight. They were probably of greasewood. A man took such a set down from their storage place in the rafters of his adobe house, saying he would miss them, as he had used them a long time and liked the shape of them. The sticks are now preserved in a museum.

An inverted basket, like that used as a drum, is commonly used in southern Arizona as a resonator for the notched stick rattle. At a Deer dance of the Yaqui the resonators were halves of gourds, placed flat on the ground. The scraping sticks were made of the rib of the sahauro cactus, about twenty-two inches long, cut with very shallow notches, and they were rasped by a slender stick of greasewood.

History of the Study of Indian Music

THE first analytical study of Indian music was made by a German and published in Germany. The man doing this work was Theodor Baker, who came to the United States in 1880, remained among the Seneca Indians of New York during the summer, and visited the United States Indian School at Carlisle, Pennsylvania. The result of this work was published two years later in a book of eighty-two pages entitled *Ueber die Musik der Nordamerikanischen Wilden*. It is said that he made the research in order to obtain a doctor's degree at the University of Leipzig, but this is not mentioned in his publication. Dr. Baker's work included transcriptions of forty-three songs, with a tabulated analysis of their structure and detailed descriptions of the musical customs of these Indians. The songs were written down by ear and in ordinary musical notation but he did not claim that the Indians sang the exact tones of the diatonic scale. He described the musical instruments used by the Indians and gave valuable data on their manner of life as well as on their songs. The gatherings of Indians attended by him were often so large that the voices of the singers could not be heard by all the people, and a stamping of the feet of the dancers was necessary "to keep the music in order."

The name of Miss Alice Cunningham Fletcher is forever linked with the music of the American Indians. Her first contribution to the subject was published in 1884 and entitled *The "Wawan" or Pipe Dance of the*

Omahas. Ten melodies were presented in this paper, which was published by the Peabody Museum of American Archæology and Ethnology at Cambridge, Massachusetts. Miss Fletcher went among the Omaha for scientific work in 1883, and early secured the assistance of Francis La Flesche, a son of the head chief, whose cooperation continued until her death in 1922. Her work became widely known through a later work which will be considered in a subsequent paragraph.

Dr. Carl Stumpf of Vienna published a pamphlet on *Lieder der Bellakula Indianer* in 1886, thus early presenting material on the Indians of British Columbia. In 1888, Dr. Franz Boas of Columbia University, New York, published twenty-three Eskimo songs with analytical notes in his work on *The Central Eskimo.* These were transcribed in ordinary musical notation, but in some instances he indicated the rhythm by accents, omitting the bars. Dr. Boas has continued his interest in Indian music up to the present time (1936) with occasional contributions to the subject in which he has stressed the importance of rhythm in primitive music.

An early and devoted student of Indian music was Carlos Troyer, who went to live among the Zuni in 1888 and was a leading exponent of popular adaptation of Indian melodies. He wrote many compositions on Indian themes and was the author of a lecture entitled "Traditional Songs of the Zuni," published in 1913. (See chapter on "Adaptations of Indian Music.")

The invention of the phonograph with its recording apparatus marked the beginning of a new era in the preservation of Indian songs. Instead of requiring the

THE STUDY OF INDIAN MUSIC

Indian to sing a song over and over so that it could be written down by ear, the student recorded it by means of the phonograph and could study the record at his leisure. The first phonographs were operated by a treadle which gave an uneven motion; later they were provided with electro-motors and storage batteries, but these, too, were unsatisfactory. The spring motor supplanted these, and the modern type of cylinder phonograph became established (see page 126).

A phonograph was used by Dr. Jesse Walter Fewkes in the winter of 1889 for recording the songs and folklore of the Passamaquoddy Indians in Maine. His description of this work, with three melodies, was published in 1890 and is believed to be the first printed account of the use of a phonograph in work among Indians. On his next visit to the Zuni, as director of the Hemenway Southwestern Expedition, he used the phonograph in recording Zuni songs and language. Two articles on his work with the phonograph among the Zuni were published by Dr. Fewkes in 1890. Mrs. Mary Hemenway, founder of the expedition, entrusted the study of these cylinder records to Dr. Benjamin Ives Gilman, who at that time was lecturing at Harvard University on the psychology of music and who later held the position of curator of the Art Museum in Boston. Dr. Gilman's scholarly treatment of this subject is contained in a paper on *Zuni Melodies* published in 1891.

The Hemenway Expedition moved from the Zuni to the Hopi villages of Arizona in 1891 and Dr. Fewkes recorded a number of Hopi songs, which were studied intensively by both Dr. Gilman and Dr. Fewkes, the former writing a book of more than two hundred

AMERICAN INDIANS AND THEIR MUSIC

pages, entitled *Hopi Songs,* which was published in 1908. This book contains seventeen songs transcribed in ordinary musical notation and also in a "phonographic notation" consisting of notes placed on eleven to twenty-four parallel lines. The trend of the melody is also shown by ascending and descending lines on similar parallels.

The book which marked the beginning of a popular interest in Indian music was written by Miss Alice Fletcher and published in 1893. This book was entitled *A Study of Omaha Indian Music,* and contained a "report on the structural peculiarities of the music" by John Comfort Fillmore. The sympathetic descriptions of Indian customs and ceremonies, as well as the presentation of the Indian songs with harmonizations, gave this book a peculiar appeal, and it won wide recognition. Some of the same songs are contained in Miss Fletcher's book, *Indian Story and Song from North America,* which was issued in 1900. In addition to transcribing the phonograph records obtained by Miss Fletcher, the work of Professor Fillmore included the transcription of eleven Navaho songs obtained by Washington Matthews and published in his book, *Navaho Legends,* in 1897. Miss Fletcher's work included the phonographic recording of songs among the Ponca, Otoe, and numerous other tribes, many of which she herself transcribed, while a portion (after the death of Professor Fillmore) were transcribed by Edwin S. Tracy. Her book on *The Hako: A Pawnee Ceremony,* contained one hundred and four melodies and was widely read. This book was published in 1904. Songs occur also in *The Omaha Tribe* by Miss Fletcher and Francis La Flesche, published in 1911.

THE STUDY OF INDIAN MUSIC

Like *The Hako*, this was published by the Bureau of American Ethnology.

Mention should once more be made of the work of Charles K. Wead (see page 96), who studied Indian music from the standpoint of a musician-physicist and contributed largely to the development of the subject.

During the last decade of the nineteenth century there were interesting contributions to Indian music in connection with the study of Indian culture. Songs were included in *The Midewiwin or Grand Medicine Society of the Ojibwa*, by Dr. Walter James Hoffman, and in *The Ghost Dance Religion*, by James Mooney. Later Dr. Franz Boas published a paper on the Kwakiutl Indians with twenty-three songs, Alexander T. Cringan wrote *Iroquois Folk Songs* and other scientists gave attention to the subject in their writings. *The Mountain Chant of the Navaho*, by Washington Matthews, published in 1902, contains transcriptions of seventeen songs which, like all songs collected during this period, were recorded on the phonograph. Among others who have given attention to Indian music in their publications are Dr. Walter Hough, Dr. John R. Swanton, Albert Samuel Gatschet, George A. Dorsey, James Owen Dorsey and Henry Rowe Schoolcraft. Henry E. Krehbiel contributed to the subject in connection with his study of folk music.

Early in the twentieth century there arose two German scientists whose names, like that of Dr. Stumpf, will always be connected with the study of Indian and exotic music. These were Dr. E. von Hornbostel and Dr. O. Abraham, and their method was based upon a minute investigation of the sounds produced by the singers. Their first publication on Indian music was issued in 1904, and their work continued until the World War, numerous pamphlets being printed during that time. Dr. von Hornbostel continued his work upon Indian music until his death in November 1935.

Side by side with this intensive study of Indian music there appeared an increasing interest in the subject from the esthetic standpoint, with a popular interest in the general subject of the Indians. Miss Natalie Curtis (later Mrs. Paul Burlin) began writing on the subject in 1903 and published *The Indians' Book* in 1907, with many Pueblo melodies and delightful descriptions of their use. Her interest in Indian music continued until her death in 1922. *American Primitive Music,* by Dr. Frederick Russell Burton, was published in 1909, and Dr. Burton wrote several magazine articles on the subject.

The present writer began her study of Indian music in 1893, through a personal acquaintance with Professor Fillmore and the reading of Miss Fletcher's book, published in that year. Her pursuit of the study was largely due, in the next few years, to Miss Fletcher's gracious kindness and encouragement. The work of a piano teacher and church organist had not brought any contact with the American Indians, but after a long course of reading on the subject she began noting down the songs of Chippewa and Sioux. In 1907 she entered upon research on Indian music for the Bureau of American Ethnology of the Smithsonian Institution, a connection continuing to the present time (1936), her position being that of a Collaborator of the Bureau. A phonograph or other recording equipment is taken to Indian reservations, and the songs recorded, together with all available information concerning their history and use. These song records are later transcribed in ordinary musical notation, and the results, in many tribes, have been published by the Bureau of Ethnology. The tribes whose music has thus been published are the Chippewa, Sioux, Ute, Mandan, Hidatsa, Pawnee, Papago, Yuma, Cocopa, Yaqui and Menominee. Two books awaiting publication at the Bureau of American Ethnology are *Nootka and Quileute Music* and *British Columbian Music*. Other unpublished material is on the music of the Winnebago, Alabama, Choctaw, Pueblo and Seminole Indians. More than 2,250 songs have been transcribed, and hundreds of additional songs have been recorded and studied without transcription. The original recordings are catalogued, and are in the possession of the Bureau of American Ethnology. During 1935 she recorded Cheyenne and Arapaho songs under the auspices of the Southwest Museum, which published a book on the subject. Further work for that museum was begun in 1936, the subject being certain Pueblo songs.

A phonograph operated by spring motor is convenient for use in the field. The writer has recorded Indian songs with a two-minute and a four-minute phonograph, an American dictaphone operated by storage battery and by city current, and also by an electrically operated disk recording apparatus. In addition to these, an ediphone with storage battery and a portable disk apparatus have been used by other investigators. Some songs recorded by the writer have been copied on disks by means of an RCA Victor, D 22, radio phonograph.

Canada, as well as the United States, has given attention to Indian music. Several interesting papers on

AMERICAN INDIANS AND THEIR MUSIC

Iroquois music by Alexander T. Cringan have been published by the Canadian government, among them a paper on Iroquois folk songs, with thirty-four melodies. A notable collection of phonograph records of Indian songs fully catalogued is in the possession of the Victoria Memorial Museum in Ottawa, Canada. These are chiefly the songs of British Columbia Indians and Eskimo, and were obtained by C. M. Barbeau, D. Jenness, J. A. Mason, J. A. Teit and others, during a period beginning in 1911. About two hundred of these songs have been transcribed by Miss Helen Heffron Roberts, and others by Dr. Jacob D. Sapir, curator of anthropology in that museum. Dr. Sapir also transcribed forty-nine ceremonial songs of the Creek and Yuchi Indians, which were collected and published by Dr. Frank G. Speck of the University of Pennsylvania. Dr. Speck recently recorded songs among the Cherokee Indians of North Carolina. Numerous investigators have added to the collections of song records in various institutions. Miss Helen H. Roberts has worked in the field of Indian music for many years. She has recorded Indian songs in California and published a portion of this material, also has transcribed Salish and Copper Eskimo songs. She was formerly connected with the Department of Anthropology of Yale University.

Dr. George Herzog, until recently connected with the Department of Anthropology at Yale University and now lecturer on Primitive Music and Primitive Languages in the same department at Columbia University, is contributing greatly to the advance of research in this field. His new book, issued by the American Council of Learned Societies and noted in the following list, contains valuable bibliographies and lists of collections of recordings of Indian and exotic music. No reference work of this sort has previously been available.

It has been possible, in this single chapter, to indicate only the principal writers on this subject and to mention their more important works. The following is a partial bibliography of titles of books, the names of publishers being obtainable from library lists. Contributions contained in periodicals are not included.

BAKER, THEODOR—*Ueber die Musik der Nordamerikanischen Wilden* - - - - - - - - - - - - 1882

FLETCHER, ALICE C.—*The "Wawan" or Pipe Dance of the Omahas* - - - - - - - - - - - - 1884

STUMPF, CARL—*Lieder der Bellakula Indianer* - - - 1886

BOAS, FRANZ—*The Central Eskimo* - - - - - - 1888

FEWKES, JESSE WALTER—*A Contribution to Passamaquoddy Folklore* - - - - - - - - - - 1890

———*On the Use of the Phonograph among the Zuni Indians* - - - - - - - - - - - - - - 1890

———*Additional Studies of Zuni Songs and Rituals with the Phonograph* - - - - - - - - - - - 1890

GILMAN, BENJAMIN IVES—*Zuni Melodies* - - - - 1891

FLETCHER, ALICE C. with FILLMORE, J. C.—*A Study of Omaha Indian Music* - - - - - - - - 1893

FLETCHER, ALICE C.—*Indian Story and Song from North America* - - - - - - - - - - - - - 1900

WEAD, CHARLES KASSON—*Contributions to the History of Musical Scales* - - - - - - - - - - - 1902

CRINGAN, ALEXANDER T.—*Iroquois Folk Songs* - - 1903

ABRAHAM, O. and HORNBOSTEL, E. V.—*Phonographierte Indische Melodien* - - - - - - - - - 1904

FLETCHER, ALICE C.—*The Hako: A Pawnee Ceremony*   1904
———with FRANCIS LA FLESCHE, *The Omaha Tribe*   1911
CURTIS, NATALIE—*The Indians' Book* - - - - -   1907
GILMAN, BENJAMIN IVES—*Hopi Songs* - - - - -   1908
BURTON, FREDERICK R.—*American Primitive Music* -   1909
DENSMORE, FRANCES—*Chippewa Music* - - - - -   1910
SPECK, F. G. with SAPIR, J. D.—*Ceremonial Songs of the Creek and Yuchi Indians* - - - - - - - -   1911
DENSMORE, FRANCES—*Chippewa Music II* - - - -   1913
TROYER, CARLOS—*Indian Music Lecture* - - - - -   1913
FLETCHER, A. C.—*Indian Games and Dances with Native Songs* - - - - - - - - - - - - - -   1915
DENSMORE, FRANCES—*Teton Sioux Music* - - - -   1918
———*Indian Action Songs* - - - - - - - -   1921
———*Northern Ute Music* - - - - - - - -   1922
———*Mandan and Hidatsa Music* - - - - - -   1923
———*Music of the Tule Indians of Panama* - - -   1926
ROBERTS, HELEN H., and JENNESS, DIAMOND.—*Songs of the Copper Eskimo* - - - - - - - - - -   1925
———Analysis of Picuris songs in J. P. HARRINGTON, *Picuris Children's Stories* - - - - - - - -   1928
DENSMORE, FRANCES—*Pawnee Music* - - - - - -   1929
———*Papago Music* - - - - - - - - - -   1929
———*Menominee Music* - - - - - - - - -   1932
———*Yuman and Yaqui Music* - - - - - - -   1932
HERZOG, GEORGE—"Maricopa Music," in L. SPIER, *Yuman Tribes of the Gila River* - - - - - - - -   1933
ROBERTS, HELEN H.—*Form in Primitive Music* - -   1933
DENSMORE, FRANCES—*Cheyenne and Arapaho Music*   1936
HERZOG, GEORGE—*Research in Primitive and Folk Music in the United States* - - - - - - - - - -   1936

Some Results of the Study of Indian Music

EACH of the students of Indian music mentioned in the preceding chapter made a definite contribution to the subject. Dr. Baker, by his tabulation of the melodies, showed the persistence of the fifth above the keynote in the songs under observation. The following quotations from his book are also of interest:

The Indians say that the songs connected with the religious concepts were of supernatural origin and that the newer songs are only imitations of these songs.

The metrical dividing of the melodies is a consequence of the rhythmical *feeling* of the natives. This is not accidental but the result of slow development.

John C. Fillmore, to whom Miss Fletcher entrusted the study of her Indian songs, was a teacher, and an exponent of the romantic school of piano music. He claimed that the Indians have a "subconscious sense of harmony," even of modulations from one key to another, stating that "folk melody, so far as now appears, is always and everywhere harmonic melody." If he had refrained from extravagance in his statements and had explained the frequency of "chord sequences of tone" by saying that the line of least resistance for the Indian voice appeared to be the upper partials (overtones) of a fundamental, he would have linked his observations, in some degree, to those of Dr. Baker. Instead, he presented the hypothesis of a complete harmonic sense, offering as proof the statement that certain Indians preferred harmonizations to the playing of their songs on an organ without accompaniment of chords, and that they preferred certain chords to others.

Dr. Gilman denied not only the sense of harmony but even the existence of a "sense of scale" among the Indians. Writing on Zuni music he said:

> What we have in these melodies is the musical growths out of which scales are elaborated, and not compositions undertaken in conformity to norms of interval order already fixed in the consciousness of the singers. In this archaic stage of art, scales are not formed but forming.

The work of Dr. Gilman was done, as indicated, with phonograph records made on the Indian reservations by Dr. Fewkes, and his method was based upon fine discrimination of pitch. Dr. Franz Boas, with a particularly wide experience among Indians, wrote in 1888, "On the whole, the melodies, even to our musical sense, can be traced to a keynote."

It is to be regretted that Miss Fletcher, by endorsing the position of Fillmore, placed herself in a position where she could not speak independently on a subject which she, more than any other observer of that time, had an opportunity to study in the field. The following statement made by Miss Fletcher in 1893 is, however, of great value.

> During the earlier years of my studies, I was, with other observers, inclined to believe in the theory of a musical scale in which the interval of a tone was divided into many parts; but, for several years now past, having become more familiar with the Indian's mode of thought and feeling concerning music, and as a result of careful investigation of hundreds of songs which

SOME RESULTS OF THE STUDY

I have transcribed, I have been led to account for his peculiar intonations in other ways than in the use of a minutely divided scale.

The present writer, early in her work, devised a system of tabulated analyses by which the characteristics of large numbers of Indian songs can be indicated in terms of percentage. From these tables it appears that a large majority of the songs, by their tonal material and progressions, suggest a fundamental tone and its simplest upper partials. There are, however, a number of songs which have no keynote in the musician's use of that term. No attempt has been made to fit these songs into any other musical system than our own. They are regarded as "pure melody without tonality" and are classified as irregular in melodic form, constituting an interesting group for further study.

In the songs with apparent keynote it is found that the octave and fifth above that tone are sung with the best intonation, the major third is usually given with clearness, the fourth and seventh are often variable in intonation, and the semitone is the most variable in pitch. The interval transcribed as a minor third is frequently a non-major rather than an exact minor third. The question of "scale" is considered in a later chapter. In regard to small divisions of a tone, the writer agrees with the above statement by Miss Fletcher.

Certain Peculiarities of Indian Music

A STATEMENT of A. H. Fox Strangways concerning the music of Hindostan is applicable to the music of the American Indians. Mr. Strangways says: "One caution with regard to these tunes. It would be a mistake to play them on a keyed instrument; they should be played on a violin, or sung, or whistled, or merely thought. Not only because there is then a hope of their being rendered in natural intonation and of getting the sharp edges of the tones rounded by some sort of portamento, but also because the temperament of a keyed instrument . . . has a unique power of making an unharmonized melody sound invincibly commonplace."[14]

All who are familiar with Indian music will admit that it loses its native character when played on a piano. An Indian may sing a tone of the same pitch as the piano but his manner of producing the tone and of passing from one tone to another is such that it cannot be imitated on any keyed instrument. The only way to preserve an Indian song so it can be generally understood is to transcribe it in the musical notation with which we are familiar, but the best way to learn an Indian song from such a transcription is to hum it, tapping the time on a table or on a heavy book. This will be found more satisfactory than playing it on a

---

[14] Strangways, A. H. Fox, *The Music of Hindostan,* Oxford, England, 1914, p. 18.

PECULIARITIES OF INDIAN MUSIC

piano, even for the purpose of memorizing it. A portion of Indian songs can be harmonized but a very large number belong to the class known as "non-harmonic music" which cannot be harmonized in a satisfactory manner.

Indian singing differs from our own in that it is not accompanied by an instrument giving gradations of pitch. The singing of the Indians is accompanied only by percussion instruments. An accompaniment of three or four drums or rattles is occasionally used but there is no definite pitch among them.

The usual comment on Indian songs is that they begin high, end low, and have more rhythm than melody. Generally speaking, this is correct. Thus in a classification of 1,553 songs,[15] containing 44,061 intervals, it was found that sixty per cent were ascending and forty per cent descending progressions; and that in sixty-eight per cent the last note was the lowest note occurring in the melody. In a song with steady downward trend the last note is not always the keynote. Sometimes a song with a compass of twelve tones begins on the ninth and ends on the fifth (keynote G, first note A, last note D, in lower octave) while others begin on the twelfth and end on the keynote (keynote G, first note D in upper octave, last note G).

It is interesting to note the contrasts between the Indian customs and our own. For example, the Indians find their greatest pleasure in chorus singing while we

---

[15] This group comprises Chippewa, Sioux, Ute, Mandan, Hidatsa, Papago, Pawnee, Menominee, Yuman, Yaqui, Nootka and Quileute songs. The tribes not yet incorporated in this cumulative analysis are the Winnebago, Seminole, Choctaw, Alabama, Cheyenne, Arapaho, Pueblo and the tribes of British Columbia.

emphasize the singing of solos. When an Indian sings alone at a public gathering it is not because he is a good singer, but because he is singing a song that belongs to him, having been "received from a spirit in a dream," or having some other personal connection. A woman may do the same, occasionally singing the war song of a deceased relative or a song composed in his honor. A doctor may sing alone when treating the sick but he often desires the family or friends of the sick person to join him, not because the sound will be more pleasing but in order that their orenda (see page 64) may supplement his own.

Indians usually sing in a large lodge or in the open air, and the voice of a "good singer" must have a carrying quality not necessary among people who sing in a comparatively small room. The singers at a dance are usually seated around a large drum, beating right lustily upon it as they sing. The leader sings the first phrase of a song softly in order that the others may identify the melody, then the others join him, usually repeating the first phrase, which has served as an introduction. In some tribes the women sing with the men, sitting in a circle a few feet behind the circle of men at the drum. Their heads are covered by their shawls and they often cover their mouths as they sing the melody an octave higher than the men, in a high, nasal tone. They are a strange circle of motionless, shrouded figures, and stranger still is the high, thin tone they produce.

Music among the Indians is essentially a man's occupation. He sings the rituals and ceremonial songs, and treats the sick. In this we find additional evidence of a belief in the power of music. Women are not expected

PECULIARITIES OF INDIAN MUSIC

to have the same power as men in accomplishing wonderful things such as bringing rain, calling the buffalo, healing the sick or talking with the spirits of the dead, although medicine women are not unknown among Indians and are highly respected.

We scarcely realize the extent to which our vocal music is based upon an imitation of a tuned instrument. Comparison with a standardized pitch is unknown among the Indians and they find pleasure in sounds which are not pleasing to our ears. Nevertheless, they have standards of musical excellence not unlike our own. For example, it is required that a good singer have a large repertory and be able to sing a song correctly after hearing it two or three times; he must also have a "convincing quality" in his work, showing a mental grasp of the song. Such a man is leader of the singers. Readiness in learning a song is especially useful when an Indian visits another tribe and wishes to carry home some songs. In my experience, the singers regarded as proficient by their own people have what we call a good intonation, using the intervals of the diatonic scale with an accuracy that would be considered acceptable in a member of our own race. This accuracy applies especially to the simpler upper partials of a fundamental.

The manner of tone production used by the Indians is peculiar to their race. The Indian sings with his teeth slightly separated and motionless, and there is very little change in the position of his lips, the tone seeming to be forced outward by an action of the muscles of his throat. An Indian said, "Something seems to go up and down in my throat when I sing." This forcing of the tone gives it remarkable carrying power. A vibrato is often cultivated and admired. In some tribes there are special qualities of tone for certain classes of songs, the love songs being sung in a peculiar nasal tone, while the lullabies are marked by an upward gliding of the voice before a rest. The Ute gaming songs are marked by an unaccented grace note before the melody tone, the voice sliding upward to the principal tone; and in the Ute songs of the Bear dance there is a sliding downward of the voice. A glissando is used in many songs. It is the custom to follow certain songs with vocables or other sounds, the "medicine songs" often being followed by "Wah——— Hee, hee, hee!" and the war songs of the Plains by a shrill "Ki, yi, yi." The Makah songs concerning the whale are always followed by a long howl, this being given after each song by the men in canoes when towing a dead whale to the shore.

The accuracy with which a song is repeated by the Indians was proved by having a song recorded at intervals of considerable time, and also by the recording of the same song by different men. For example, an old man recorded a song in the summer and again in the following winter. A comparison of the two records showed the melody, pitch and tempo to be identical. A similar accuracy was found in songs recorded by a woman after a lapse of three years, the two sets of records being exactly alike. A song is frequently sung eight or even ten times on a phonograph cylinder and the renditions are uniform in every respect. The only exception occurs in songs having several "verses" in which the lengths of the tones vary somewhat with the words. In certain tribes there is a rigid requirement of accuracy in ceremonial songs. If a mistake is made the

PECULIARITIES OF INDIAN MUSIC

ceremony must be begun over again and the unfortunate singer must pay a heavy fine. If a man should pretend to know a song and sing it badly he would be severely ridiculed by his people.

The number of songs in the repertory of an Indian is remarkable. I have heard of an Indian who can sing all night for three or four nights, singing each song only four times and not repeating a single song. It is said that many men know three hundred or four hundred songs. I have never tested an Indian to this extent but have recorded more than 200 songs from one singer without any sign of reaching the end of his memory. This is the more astonishing as the Indians have no system of musical notation. The only approach to this is a system of picture-writing in which the Chippewa record the words of the songs of their Grand Medicine Society, a secret organization. There are certain symbols which represent words occurring in the songs, and by the grouping of these symbols the initiated Indian knows what song is intended. He recalls the melody by looking at these little pictures. The songs are in groups of ten, and a member of the society has little strips of birch bark on which are the pictures of the songs, always sung in the same order (see page 22).

Very old songs are highly regarded by the Indians and are handed down from one generation to another. Even at the present time the age of a song is reckoned by generations of men, a singer saying that the song belonged to his grandfather or his great-grandfather. It is said that all the old songs were "received in dreams" (see page 79) while modern songs are "com-

[139]

posed." Only in a very few tribes are songs being received in the old way at the present time.

The rhythm of Indian songs is characterized by accents which are not evenly spaced, as in songs of the white race, but occur in what often appears to be an irregular manner. When a song is transcribed, a bar is placed before each accented tone and the space between the bars is considered a measure, whether it contains two or five counts and regardless of the number of counts in the measures preceding and following. The Indian sings the rhythm of a song as it was taught to him, but the present writer uses bars and measures because they make the transcription more intelligible. A large majority of Indian songs contain these changes of measure-lengths. At first these changes of time seem erratic, but when the song is regarded as a whole, and especially when it becomes familiar, the changes of measure-lengths are merged in a rhythmic unity which is interesting and satisfactory.

Many Indian songs are thematic in character, one or two themes being worked over in somewhat the same manner that a composer of our own race works over a theme and develops it. In other songs a unit of rhythm is repeated without change throughout the melody. A simple pattern is seen in a song containing four periods of equal or nearly equal length, the rhythm of the first, second and last being the same, while the third period is slightly different. In many Indian songs there is a slight change or "catch" in the rhythm soon after the middle of the song. There are, however, many songs whose rhythm cannot be divided into phrases or periods, the entire song being a rhythmic whole. In a small proportion of songs there is a

PECULIARITIES OF INDIAN MUSIC

change of tempo, occurring at the same place in all renditions. Some songs are sung with a slight rubato but the Indian usually maintains a metric unit with remarkable regularity, whatever may be the accents in the song.

In addition to the foregoing general characteristics of Indian songs there are tribal characteristics, one tribe differing from another in the structure of its songs. The Pawnee songs are lacking in melodic variety, while the Papago songs are tuneful. The Menominee songs are more pleasing and varied than the Chippewa, and the Makah songs are characterized by a small compass, many having a range of only four tones. The songs of the Yuma, Papago, Yaqui and Makah contain more songs without apparent keynote than the songs of other tribes studied by the present writer, these songs being regarded as pure melody without tonality. Indians recognize differences in musical ability among the tribes, saying that such-and-such a tribe "sings a great deal and has good songs."

Tribes differ in the use of rests. Thus in three hundred and forty Chippewa songs there is scarcely a rest, and one wonders how and where the singer takes breath in the long melodies; while in the Cocopa and certain other tribes the rests are frequent and are clearly given in all renditions of the songs. The songs of the Seminole contained a "period formation" found also among the Choctaw in Mississippi and the Tule Indians of Panama. This occurred in a few of the oldest songs, and was also found in Yuman and Pueblo songs.

A large majority of male voices among the Indians

are baritone in range, while the voices of the women usually are alto or contralto in compass, sometimes extending down to E, third space in the bass clef. The song with largest compass recorded by the writer is a Sioux song with a range of seventeen tones. The songs connected with the playing of games are usually smaller in compass than other classes of songs and contain short phrases, separated by short rests.

It is interesting to note a statement by Major John Wesley Powell, Director of the Bureau of American Ethnology at the time of its organization. Dr. Powell regarded rhythm as the first element of music and assigned it to the "hunter stage" of man's development, stating that "passing from the hunter stage to the shepherd stage we find that a new element is added to music; then melody appears fully fledged. . . . So music was endowed first with rhythm and then with melody." It appears to the writer that the elaboration of rhythm is an early phase of music as a cultivated art among primitive people.

Scale in Indian Music

A CONSIDERATION of Indian music would be incomplete without a reference to the mooted question of whether Indian music is based upon "our scale" or whether the Indians have a scale of their own.

Everyone who listens to the singing of the Indians will hear gradations of sound different from the pitch of a piano, which is accepted as a convenient standard, but that is far from indicating that the Indians have a definite scale, with minutely divided intervals like that of some oriental peoples (see pages 132-133). There is nothing in the general culture of the Indians to suggest that they would create a complicated, highly developed tonal system like that of the Hindu and the Chinese. The Indian trains his ear to catch sounds that we fail to notice, but there is no evidence that he trains his ear to detect small differences in the pitch of tones in his songs. If he were a master of small gradations in pitch we should not find, as we do find, that he varies a semitone more than any other interval in his singing and that he seldom sings a succession of whole tones accurately. He seems unable to repeat a succession of tones on one pitch, such a succession showing variations both upward and downward. By contrast, the large intervals of a major third, a fifth and an octave are generally sung with what any musician would call good intonation.

What do we mean by "our scale"? Presumably we mean the major and harmonic or melodic minor. The diatonic scale was not introduced into our musical system until the sixteenth century and is based on the laws of sound—the great underlying law being that of the upper partials of a fundamental tone. If we speak of "the pentatonic scale" we may refer to either the major or the minor pentatonic which can be played on the black keys of a piano. Helmholtz designated five pentatonic scales in which each of the black keys becomes a keynote. All these five scales have been found in Indian songs, as shown in my tabulated analyses. Many other Indian songs contain five tones of the octave, but these cannot be said to constitute a "scale." The Hindu have several hundred pentatonic scales, each with a different name. Until we can agree upon a clear definition of the word "scale" it seems advisable to avoid it when describing Indian music. There are many Indian songs in which a key is established, in the common use of that term, and others in which the tones of a key are present but their sequence is not such as fully to establish the key. In some songs the melody ends on a whole tone above the tone which, in the course of the melody, has appeared to be the keynote. In studying Indian songs we are dealing with primitive material, and the terms current in civilization are used only for convenience, to indicate the observation as nearly as possible.

The three principal melodic structures noted by the writer are (1) a structure suggesting a consciousness of the overtones of a fundamental, (2) a structure based upon tetrachords, complete and incomplete, and (3) a peculiar melodic formation with small compass in which the melody is based on one tone, stepping cautiously to one or two tones above or below that pivotal tone. The regional distribution of these melodic patterns suggests a survival of foreign influences at a remotely early time.

The rhythmic formation of melodies in short phrases, in a rhythm of the song as a whole, and in long periods repeated in a formal order, is apart from present consideration.

Although the large majority of Indian songs appear to have a keynote, they belong to the class of music known as "non-harmonic." For that reason they lose their native character when accompanied by a piano. This has been noted in the folk songs of many other peoples. Dr. Ivan Zoch, who studied Slavic music more than forty years ago, was impressed with the fact that most Slavic folk songs cannot be accompanied on the piano, so he developed a twelve-tone scale and laid it out on a monochord. A piano was tuned according to this scale but, like many other experiments, it represented a theory which could not be proved. Dr. Max Meyer presented a theory of instinctive progressions of melody and constructed a reed organ with twenty-nine tone-degrees to the octave, but this also led to no permanent results. The theories of civilization cannot catch the native element in the music of primitive peoples.

Dr. C. J. Sharp, in his study of English folk song, has called attention to the fact that it is communal and the product of a race rather than an individual. He has done a service to all students of natural melody by insisting that such songs cannot be harmonized without sacrificing their charm. The same is urged by A. H. Fox Strangways in his study of the music of Hindostan.

In conclusion, it is hoped that Indian music will be studied as an expression different from our own music, and that the native elements will be considered more important than a comparison with our own musical system.

Adaptations of Indian Music

THE first adaptations of Indian music were contained in Miss Fletcher's book *A Study of Omaha Indian Music,* published in 1893. Prof. Fillmore harmonized the songs of the Omaha and neighboring tribes collected by Miss Fletcher and presented some in four-part harmony, similar to hymns, others with an accompaniment of simple chords, and others with octaves or chords in the bass marked with accents to represent the sound of the drum. Arpeggio chords and a tremolo of octaves or chords occurred in some of these harmonizations. The melody, with the Indian words, formed the upper or soprano part, and in some instances two signatures (or keys) are indicated in the same song. There are frequent changes of measure-lengths in accordance with the accenting of the melody by the Indian singer.

The first arrangements of Indian songs with typical piano accompaniment were the work of Carlos Troyer, who, as already stated, went to live among the Zuni in 1888. Troyer introduced Indian songs to the concert platform, paraphrasing the words of the Indian song or describing an Indian custom in simple verse and writing an accompaniment in the accepted form. His verse was usually in regular rhythm and as Indian songs are irregularly accented it appears probable that the Indian melodies were changed to fit the meter of the poem. The popularity of Troyer's work assisted greatly in arousing a general interest in Indian music, and some of his songs are favorites at the present time. Troyer died in 1920.

Several songs collected by Natalie Curtis were arranged for choruses as well as for solo voices. Dr. Frederick R. Burton is known chiefly by his adaptations of Ojibwa airs. His standpoint was that of a composer in search of material and his book entitled *American Primitive Music* contains twenty-eight songs, the most familiar being "My Bark Canoe."

In 1902 there was instituted at Newton Center, Massachusetts, an enterprise intended to "promote by publication and public hearing the most progressive, characteristic and serious works of American composers, known or unknown, and to present compositions based on the melodies and folklore of the American Indians." This was "organized and directly conducted by composers," the leader of the enterprise being Arthur Farwell, who also lectured on Indian music. The name "Wawan Press" was taken from the Omaha word *wawan* which means "to sing to," and had become somewhat familiar through Miss Fletcher's description of the Wawan ceremony. Many interesting compositions were published by the Wawan Press, a large number being based on themes collected by Miss Fletcher. A majority of these compositions were by Farwell and Harvey Worthington Loomis.

Edward MacDowell's *Indian Suite* is his only contribution to this subject and its thematic material, at least in part, was taken from Indian sources. Arthur Nevin collected musical material among the Blackfoot Indians in Montana in 1903-1904, and his opera *Poia*, based on the Sun legend of the Blackfoot, was produced at the Royal Opera in Berlin in 1910.

The two composers whose work upon Indian themes is most familiar are Charles Wakefield Cadman and Thurlow Lieurance. The former based his earlier work upon themes collected by Miss Fletcher and Dr. Burton, and began his personal experience with Indians by visiting the Omaha reservation in 1909 and obtaining songs direct from the Indians. This experience he has extended to the Pueblo and other tribes. Lieurance began his acquaintance with Indians on the Crow reservation in Montana and has gathered material in many tribes. He has made a study of Indian flutes and collected many of these instruments.

No composer in this field has produced works of greater dignity than Dr. Carl Busch of Kansas City. His compositions on Indian themes extend over a long term of years and are written chiefly for orchestra, and for chorus with orchestral accompaniment.

Among other composers who have used Indian themes are Victor Herbert, John Philip Sousa, Homer Grun, C. Orem, F. A. Grant-Schaeffer, C. S. Skilton, E. A. Mueller, Robert Rochelle, William Lester, A. Herman, M. L. Lake, D. Wheelock, J. Lewis Brown, Eastwood Lane, John W. Metcalf, Horace A. Miller, Alfred Manger, Heinrich Hammer, Henry Pabst, John Mokrejs, Bessie M. Whiteley, Paul Bliss, Jean Allard Jeancon, Robert Elmer Smith, and Alfred Pochon of the Flonzaley Quartet. An Indian opera entitled *Olglala,* by Francesco De Leone, was produced in 1924, and an opera entitled *Winona,* by Alberto Bimboni, based upon Chippewa melodies, was presented in 1927-28.

Numerous pamphlets of Indian songs harmonized for use in schools and missionary meetings have been published, among them being *North American Indian Folklore Music,* prepared by the Rev. Wm. Brewster Humphrey, the harmonic arrangements of the eight melodies being by himself and Mr. S. N. Penfield. Arrangements of Indian songs are now available for use in schools and in pageants.

The number of adaptations of Indian music is so large and is growing so steadily that it is not considered expedient to include a list in the present work. Our composers are showing an appreciation of the fact that the old Indian, taking his music with him, is passing into the Great Silence.